GETTING THERE REALLY CAN BE HALF THE FUN!

Quick! What are your favorite vacation memories? The out-of-the-way inn covered with roses? The back-road cafe with home-made pastries? The picnic on the quiet hilltop away from crowds and tour buses? If this sounds good to you, you'll love touring Great Britain and Ireland on your bike. Designed to take you to the most exciting destinations via the loveliest routes, this guide will let you take control of your vacation. You'll travel when and where *you* want—and you'll do it in one of the healthiest ways possible, over some of the most spectacular cycling terrain the world has to offer.

Drawn from the authors' experiences on bicycle trips through the U.K., *Bicycle Tours of Great Britain and Ireland* tells you everything you need to know to make your trek the most exhilarating trip of your life.

- Why BYOB (Bringing Your Own Bike) is the *best* way to go
- Where to find comfortable accommodations in *every* price range
- Warm-ups to prepare you for each day's ride
- Which routes are best suited to your interests—and your physical condition
- What makes the infamous British weather a boon to bicyclists (Actually, London enjoys more sunny days per year than Rome!)
- Plus, money-saving tips for traveling at leisure and resting in comfort—no matter what season of the year you choose to go!

GAY and KATHLYN HENDRICKS are psychologists who practice and teach in Colorado. They are also avid travelers who have toured all over the world on their bikes.

BICYCLE TOURS

TOURS

—— OF ——

GREAT BRITAIN AND IRELAND

GAY & KATHLYN HENDRICKS

BICYCLE TOURS

—— OF ——

GREAT BRITAIN AND IRELAND

A PLUME BOOK

PLUME
Published by the Penguin Group
Penguin Books USA Inc., 375 Hudson Street, New York, New York 10014, U.S.A.
Penguin Books Ltd, 27 Wrights Lane, London W8 5TZ, England
Penguin Books Australia Ltd, Ringwood, Victoria, Australia
Penguin Books Canada Ltd, 10 Alcorn Avenue,
Toronto, Ontario, Canada M4V 3B2
Penguin Books (N.Z.) Ltd, 182–190 Wairau Road, Auckland 10, New Zealand

Penguin Books Ltd, Registered Offices:
Harmondsworth, Middlesex, England

First published by Plume,
an imprint of New American Library,
a division of Penguin Books USA Inc.

First Printing, April, 1992
1 3 5 7 9 10 8 6 4 2

 REGISTERED TRADEMARK—MARCA REGISTRADA

LIBRARY OF CONGRESS CATALOGING IN PUBLICATION DATA:

Hendricks, Gay
  Bicycle tours of Great Britain and Ireland / Gay and Kathlyn Hendricks.
    p. cm.
  ISBN 0–452–26772–2
  1. Bicycle touring—Great Britain—Guide-books. 2. Bicycle touring—Ireland —Guide-books. 3. Great Britain—Description and travel—1971– —Guide-
books. 4. Ireland—Description and travel—1981– —Guide-books. I. Hendricks, Kathlyn. II. Title.
GV1046.G7H46 1992
796.'4'0941—dc20   91–38679
                                                                 CIP

Printed in the United States of America
Set in Times Roman

Designed by Steven N. Stathakis

NOTE

The authors have accepted no complimentary rooms, meals, or gifts throughout any of the tours described in this book. Similarly, we have not traveled with or on any gift equipment of any kind. Therefore, you can be assured that our recommendations are based solely on personal opinion. Likewise, any opinions we express are solely our responsibility.

CONTENTS

PART TWO: THE TOURS

WARNING!

Bicycling is a strenuous sport. Before embarking on these tours, it is advisable to check with your physician to make sure you are in sound enough health to cope with the rigors of several hours of physically demanding exercise a day.

PART ONE

MAKING YOUR TOUR A SUCCESS

TOURING GREAT
BRITAIN AND IRELAND
BY BICYCLE

THE BRITISH ISLES ARE WONDERFUL PLACES TO TRAVEL, and there is no better way to do it than by bicycle. We have toured this part of the world four separate times over the last decade and have never tired of it. The people are friendly, there are plenty of bike-sized roads, and there are lots of places to stay in all budget ranges. The scenery is glorious, with the bonus of opportunities for historical learning around almost every curve.

The one thing that often stops people from touring the British Isles is that notorious weather. There is an old saying that the reason England has gone to war so often is because the men are ready and willing to escape England's climate and cooking. Yes, the weather is unpredictable, but after many years of happy touring around all parts of England, we have good news to report. We have rarely been stopped by the weather for more than a day. The rain in that part of the world often comes in showers rather than drenching down-pours. Most people would think that Rome is a sunnier city than London, but in fact, London has less annual rainfall than its Mediterranean cousin. In addition, sometimes a rainy day can be a real boon. It gives you a good excuse to spend a day in bed sipping tea, or prowling around some fascinating castle that you might not otherwise have visited. So, while we won't urge you to fill your bags with extra sunscreen, we beg you not to let fear of getting wet keep you from touring the British Isles by bicycle.

The food is a different story. After several years of experimenting, we have learned some creative ways to find consistently good meals in the U.K. More than once we have found ourselves marveling at how, with only 20 miles of water between them, there could be such a difference in the English and French approach to cooking. There is hope, however. There is a new wave of health consciousness slowly spreading over England. Many more options abound for the vegetable fanciers. Lots of salad bars and vegetarian restaurants are springing up all over England. Also, Indian and Pakistani immigration has made it possible to get superb curries and other Eastern exotica even in smaller towns. (There will be more on all this later in the book.)

FOUR GREAT REASONS TO GO

Secure in the knowledge that you won't become waterlogged or starve, let's go on to talk about some of the charms of the British Isles. The number one reason to tour Great Britain by bicycle is that you will meet unforgettable, wonderful people. We've hardly ever gone a day on our various tours without meeting some unusual, friendly person. And often we've met a roomful of them, spending an evening or a rainy afternoon in some out-of-the-way pub. There is something of the finest of humanity present whether you are deciphering the brogue of an Irishwoman, listening to an ad hoc Welsh choir, or chatting up someone you meet pedaling along a country lane. Once, for example, we were cycling along the shores of Loch Ness, home of the legendary sea monster. It was a chilly day in September, and we pulled up to rest for a few minutes.

Down at the water's edge we met a sixtyish man sitting on a stool, studying the lake. "Looking for Nessie?" we asked. "Aye," he nodded not taking his eyes off the lake. "Seen anything?" we wondered. "Nay," he said, with a perfectly straight face, "I personally think it's too cold for her today." We left him to his vigil and took to the road again.

The second great reason to tour Great Britain is for the historical wonders it affords. Nowhere will you find so much history packed into such a small area. One day you can pedal through Shakespeare's birthplace; a few days later you can ride across a windswept plain and watch Stonehenge appear on the horizon. There are treasures in store for castle lovers, cathedral fans, garden enthusiasts, and museum mavens. Bicycling is the sensible way to study all these sites, because you will be grateful for a leg-stretching walk when you park your bike outside. Plus, there are many treasures that are hidden down tiny country lanes that you would never venture into with a car. One day, for example, while riding down a tiny lane, we came upon an arrangement of prehistoric stones that covered an acre of deserted pasture. It did not appear on the map, but here it was: a record of our Druid ancestors' religious vision, spread out before us, free for the visiting.

The third good reason to visit is the glorious physical beauty of the scenery. We have laid out our tours through the very best that the British Isles have to offer. Mountain, lake, stream, and glade: you'll find them all here in profusion. The Isles have the most restful scenery we have ever toured. Sheep dot the faraway fells, a lone walker strides along a lane, a still lake beckons a reflective pause. The scenery throughout the six tours we describe rivals anything in the rest of the world.

The fourth and final reason we will mention to visit Great Britain is, believe it or not, the pubs. We are not by any means big drinkers; a glass of wine or a quick beer is plenty. But whether or not you enjoy a drink, you must experience the British pub. You can spend a wonderful evening in a pub without taking a sip of alcohol, and no one will think it odd. British pubs have an entirely different feel from American bars; they are impossible to compare to anything else. Part family, part friends, part neighborhood camaraderie, the pubs are one of the most important British institutions. It is hard to imagine Great Britain without its pubs. We always head right for the pubs as soon as we get to the British Isles. They are the best entertainment value anywhere. For the price of a beer you can spend an evening playing darts, hearing the music of language, and melting into the comfortable ambience of a strange but utterly friendly culture. Enjoy!

A SAMPLE DAY OF TOURING

Not long ago we spent what we considered a perfect day of touring. See if you would like it.

We awoke in a rambling farmhouse high on a hill in the Lake District. We had cruised into town the day before—with no reservations, as is our custom. Simply riding along looking for bed-and-breakfast signs (we saw many), we had finally chosen the establishment with the most commanding view. This meant that it was way up a hill, which had required some huffing and puffing to get there, but the friendly hostess had soon had a cup of tea and a piece of cake for us, as we sat in her living room before a crackling fire. The price for the night's lodging and breakfast, she told us, would be £10 each, the equivalent of less than $40 for both of us. After a light dinner and a couple of hours' reading we had conked out early and slept soundly until 7:30 the next morning.

Our host was a former colonel in the British army, and he could have played the part in the movies. Tall and ramrod straight, with an impressive white mustache, the only thing that detracted from his military bearing was the apron he wore as he cooked breakfast. It was in the second week of that particular tour, and we were getting a little tired of the traditional English breakfast. The classic English breakfast consists of bacon and fried eggs, with toast and, inexplicably, a fried tomato. To avoid confronting any more fried tomatoes we had asked our hosts the night before if there were any other alternatives available.

The colonel, therefore, set before us a very different but

much more delicious (to us) English breakfast. It was a bowl of porridge, with cream and a little sugar, and a plate of local field mushrooms. The mushrooms were just-picked and sautéed in butter, with that earthy, rich, meaty flavor that the fungus fancier craves. Although our hosts fretted that we weren't going to have enough energy to get through the day, we assured them that we were very happy. After breakfast we relaxed for a while on the front porch, which looked out over a valley with Lake Windermere in the distance. We were so comfortable that we decided on the spot to stay an extra day.

Midmorning, we set out to explore some of the local territory. A few miles up the road we parked and walked to the top of the highest peak in the region, which gave us a panoramic view of the Lake District. By the time we got back to town it was afternoon, but we were still full from breakfast so we decided to skip lunch. Instead we strolled around town and ended up with a lengthy browsing session and conversation with the owner in the local bookstore. We found a comfortable old tearoom for an afternoon snack. Following scones and tea we headed back up for a nap. Then, as evening came on we headed down to the pub, having done some research with the locals on which one was best. When we came in the door we knew we had found the right one. The owner was wearing a kilt, and he was in the process of telling a ring of regulars some wild tale. "Come in," he roared. "You'll be gettin' here just in time f'r th' punch line." Soon we were in the thick of things, taking on the local champion at darts (we went down to humiliating defeat). Although we fancy ourselves pretty fair competitors on the dartboard, this guy tossed one bull's-eye after another despite a state of considerable inebriation. We bought the regulars and the barkeep a round of the local bitter, which elevated us to new heights of regard in their eyes. After a couple of hours of high spirits, during which we had consumed one beer apiece, we said good night and headed off to bed. So much for the famous English reserve.

Speaking of which, the traditional joke goes like this: A group of English, Irish, Welsh, and Scots were marooned on a desert island. After two days the Scots had set up a distillery and the Irish had become their best customers. After three days the Welsh had formed a choir. Six weeks later the English were still waiting to be introduced. Like many jokes, there is a bit of truth in this story. You will find the English less voluble than their Scottish, Welsh, or Irish kin, but much of the time their reserve is just a surface manifestation. We have found that if we take time and genuinely listen, the ice melts and soon we're talking like friends.

If after reading our description of a sample day you are ready to start making plans, your first decision is when to go. After four or five different touring vacations in the British Isles, we have developed our own prejudices, which we will be happy to share with you.

WHEN TO GO

Traditionally, the season of touring in the U.K. begins in the middle of April and runs through mid-October. July and August are the two months when you find the heaviest concentration of locals on their vacations. They will often have laid claim to the best "digs," sometimes months in advance, so bicycle touring is a little more difficult in these peak months.

Here are average Fahrenheit temperatures for two key zones of the U.K.:

	APRIL	MAY	JUNE	JULY	AUGUST	SEPTEMBER	OCTOBER
London	55	63	68	70	70	66	61
Edinburgh	52	57	63	64	64	61	54

As you can see, Edinburgh lags about a month behind London and never quite catches up. If you are starting a long tour early in the season, in April for example, and you wish to take advantage of the best weather, it would be wise to tour the South first, then head up toward Scotland as it warms up. But there are advantages to every season: In spring, the green of England is at its most intense; in the fall, the hillsides of Scotland and the moors of the North are gloriously in color.

Our own favorite months are May and September. In May you beat the crowds and have the ever-pleasant natives at their most cordial. You have deep greens nearly everywhere, and the greatest likelihood of good weather. We have done tours of the U.K. in May and have been inconvenienced by bad weather. September is also fine, though by then the tourist infrastructure will have grown tired of dealing with the public. Surliness, of the kind you will sometimes encounter in France and Italy, is virtually unknown in Great Britain, so you don't have to worry much about being treated rudely. In fact, on a recent tour we stopped to ask directions of some of the scruffiest spike-haired punkers on the planet and found even them to be unfailingly polite and helpful.

To summarize, our recommendation would be to choose May, September, and then June (in that order of preference) for your touring.

WHAT KIND OF TOUR SHOULD YOU TAKE?

Going solo versus taking a group tour is a personal decision. Our personal preference now is to go solo, but in the beginning we took a couple of guided tours and are glad we did. We didn't have this book back then, and it was helpful to have someone else handling the logistics and making the decisions. The advantages of a group are primarily ease and sociability. You have a leader to handle the details, which definitely take some time and planning, no matter how efficient you are. There is a vehicle to carry the heavier luggage and provide backup service should disaster or fatigue strike. Riding a bike with loaded panniers is very different from simply carrying your camera and a tube of sunscreen. In addition, there are usually a dozen or more cyclists on a tour, and this can make for some good ready-made social times. There will always be people to eat with and go dancing with. For singles, this can be the decisive issue in choosing solo versus group travel. However, there are disadvantages to groups, too. It is statistically likely that out of a dozen or so people there are going to be a few you don't like or who don't like you. Bicycling brings out the best in people, but it can sometimes bring out the worst, especially over time. Those whiny people who mildly irritated you on the first day can make you want to brain them with your pump on the eighth.

Cost may be a big factor in your decision. Organized tours cost around $200 a day—the exact figure depends on how luxurious or spartan the tour is. For a one-week tour, then, you will be in for around $1500 plus airfare and some other expenses on either end. With a little planning, you can *easily* cut this figure in half if you go solo. If you go as a pair or even a foursome, you can shave even more dollars off your expenses. We like the freedom that going solo affords us. We can make last-minute route changes, be lazy for a morning if we choose, or do any of the many other things that come to us when we're on the road. We disliked the regimentation of the group tours we were on, but even so, we have many fond memories of some of the times we had. If you want to try a group tour, look in the back of one of the bicycling magazines (*Bicycling* is a good one) and check through the many companies listed who offer tours of the British Isles. Several reputable companies are listed at the end of our book. All of them will be happy to send you a brochure.

HOW TO GET THERE

Most travelers to England usually come into Gatwick or Heathrow, the latter being one of the busiest airports in the world. It was also once one of the most efficient, but terrorism has hampered this in recent years. Security checks have added much time to check-ins. It's fun to sit in the waiting areas and observe the passing parade of turbans, dashikis, robes, and fezzes. You may also find yourself routed into Gatwick, a smaller airport on the other side of town. From Gatwick there is a direct train to Victoria Station that leaves frequently. From Heathrow you can take the Underground to any station, all for a very modest price.

It is a good idea to shop around to find out which airlines have the best arrangements for transporting your bike to the U.K. It would be impossible for us to list the rules in this book, because airlines change them in the blink of an eye. All airlines will take your bike, though some will charge you a fee in the neighborhood of $15–25. Rules also fluctuate as to whether or not your bike will need to be boxed. Most airlines say you have to box your bike, although we have seen this rule waived on a slow day. A bike box may be obtained, usually free, from a good bike shop. In order to make the bike fit, you will need to remove the pedals, lower the seat, and turn the handlebars sideways. If you are the proverbial mechanical idiot, this operation will take you a couple of run-throughs to master. We would recommend doing a dry run before you get to the airport.

GETTING AROUND THE U.K. BY TRAIN

A blessing for the bicyclist, British Rail (or B.R. as it is widely called) is a fast, efficient rail service that goes everyplace we have ever wanted to go. The system has a wider variety of service than its European counterparts, meaning that you can go to smaller destinations by rail, but its amenities may not be as well maintained. You will find tattered seat covers on some trains, which you would never find in a Swiss railcar, and you will be served absolutely execrable tea. In fact, the only bad tea we have ever had in England is on the trains. But all in all, the system works admirably. The English are enthusiastic train riders (the rails seem to thaw some of their famous reserve), and you will always be able to get up a conversation among your fellow passengers. Best of all, the English have a much easier system for handling bicycles than their Continental counterparts. Almost always you will be able simply to take your bike back to a baggage car, lock it up yourself, then collect it when you get where you are going.

On the major routes the B.R. now has Inter-City 125s, so called because they go that many miles per hour. Hats off to the British for not charging any more for these fast trains than they do for the pokiest old locomotive. The French, for example, tack a hefty premium on the price of the ticket if you want to go fast on one of their TGVs, but the English either have not caught onto this idea or have chosen not to do it. As an example of how fast you can get from place to place on the 125s, we left London one morning at ten o'clock and were in Edinburgh, a distance of nearly 400 miles, at half past two that afternoon. On a previous trip this same journey had taken all day.

On several occasions we have booked trips on sleepers, and experienced a great deal of enjoyment. The sleeping-car trains generally have better amenities than other trains, notably bigger bathrooms and more room for your bike and luggage. You can order your breakfast in advance, and an attendant will knock on your door with it the next morning. Sleepers tend to book up early, though, so if you want one you will probably have to make advance reservations. They also cost extra.

We have always taken advantage of the BritRail Pass, which offers passes in several denominations, including one-week and two-week options. The BritRail Pass costs less than single tickets, and you are able to save some time with each transaction. Remember, however, that you cannot purchase a BritRail Pass once you get to the U.K. It must be done from outside the country. Your travel agent can help you, or you can write directly to BritRail Travel International Inc., 1500 Broadway, New York, NY 10036.

RENTING OR BUYING A BICYCLE IN THE U.K.

Many of you, like the authors, will have romantic feelings about "English bikes" from childhood. For us, they were the first thin-tired bikes with gears that we ever rode. After riding the weighty, gut-busting balloon-tired one-speeds that were popular back when we were growing up, in the '40s and '50s, English bikes seemed like heaven to ride. Nowadays, however, English bikes, with a few rare exceptions, are not as good as equipment from other countries like Japan, the U.S., and Italy. In addition, you will find prices are higher in England than for similar equipment in the U.S. So, unless you have some overriding reason for doing so, we cannot recommend that you buy a bike in England.

A similar caveat must be given about renting bikes in the U.K. We have tried it a number of times, with mixed but largely negative results. Once in Inverness, the gateway city to the Scottish highlands, we scoured every place in town that rented bikes. We didn't find anything that was fun or even safe to ride; everything we tried had something wrong with it. Finally we ended up on a couple of clunkers that served us for a few days, but which were definitely a chore to keep on the road. On another occasion, however, we found an excellent shop in Cambridge which rented us fine, sturdy three-speeds that met our needs very well for the several days we were in the vicinity. Renting bicycles tends to be quite expensive in the U.K., as it is nearly every place in the Western world.

We will not give specific recommendations on which shops have bikes for rent. The simple fact is that this information would soon be out of date, due to the rapid turnover of bicycle shops. From one tour to the next we found about half the shops had closed, moved, or quit renting bikes. Others had sprung up. The best way to rent a bike is to check with the tourist information office wherever you find yourself. They will always have the latest information about where to obtain a rental. The Raleigh Company has a Rent-A-Bike program in a hundred or so locations around the U.K. Our recommendation would be to check several places, if there are that many in the city or town you are in, because we have found that the quality ranges widely. Many years ago, before our first trip to England (not a bike trip), we read an article about how easy it was to rent bikes in the U.K. The article was cheerful, enthusiastic, and seemingly helpful. So we took it with us, thinking it would be fun to do some biking. The article had obviously been written by a public relations person instead of a cyclist, though, because most of the information turned out to be utterly erroneous. We would go to an address listed as a bike rental shop, only to find that they had never rented bikes and did not plan to. We would go to another shop and find that they once had rented bikes but had discontinued the service. So it went. As you can tell, we are not big fans of renting bikes, but if you must, check with the tourist information office.

WHAT KIND OF BICYCLE IS BEST FOR TOURING?

This question is clearly unanswerable because it is a matter of taste. We will, however, be happy to state our taste. In recent years nearly all our touring has been done on mountain bikes. We find fat-tired bikes a lot more comfortable for long-distance riding as well as for short bursts. We really have not had the kind of sore-back problems that we used to have on regular touring bikes since we started riding mountain bikes. There is no question that mountain bikes are heavier and somewhat slower, but we have found that the comfort makes up for it. The second reason we like touring on mountain bikes is the increased flexibility they give us. It is very tempting to be able to jump off-road now and then for some dirt-road touring. A third reason is practicality: We almost never have breakdowns with mountain bikes. These machines can really take a beating. It seemed when we were riding mostly thin-tired bikes that we were always fixing something, and we are not particularly enthusiastic or skilled mechanics. Very rarely does a flat tire inconvenience us anymore, whereas we averaged a flat a week when we rode thin-tired bikes. For us, then, the preference is clear, and, based on the experience of the last five years or so, growing stronger.

LODGING AND DINING OPTIONS

The British Isles are full of great places to stay, and if you look hard, you can find some great places to eat, too. Our preference is for the family-run bed and breakfast although there are lots of other options. We think the B&B is a fine institution, particularly in Great Britain, for several reasons. First of all, since they are almost always family-run, the people have a strong interest in making sure you are welcome. We have spent many evenings by the fire, talking to the owners of our lodgings or simply watching TV with them. We will always remember sitting in a Scottish farm cottage many years ago, watching the famous episode of "Dallas" where it was revealed who shot J.R. Our hosts were shocked that we had never seen "Dallas" before; they watched it every week. They were also amazed and somewhat disbelieving when we told them that "Dallas" was not an accurate picture of life in the U.S. We can truly say that we have met the warmest, most wonderful people in all our travels in English B&Bs. Nowadays, bed and breakfast establishments have gone big-time. There are lots of them, and even some chains of them. Being adventurous people, we never make reservations, preferring to take our chances. Sometimes this practice has led to the owner of a full B&B calling Aunt Martha to put us up in her spare bedroom, but we have yet to have to sleep out in the cold (or even in a barn). If you want the security of a reservation, you can have your pick of several excellent B&B guides to the U.K. A middle-ground option is to stay at one B&B, then get the owner to call ahead for you to reserve a place at the next town you'll be visiting. Most will be happy to do that for the price of the phone call.

A second reason for going the B&B route is the ease of

storing your bicycle. There will always be plenty of room to put your machines in the garage or some other safe place for the night, whereas hotels, especially in larger cities, can sometimes be shirty about bike travelers.

The third reason for using B&Bs is that they are a good bargain. On our first trip to England, nearly ten years ago, we didn't have much money. That's where we developed our taste for B&Bs, and it's never really left us.

Unless you make other arrangements, you can expect the basic English breakfast in the morning. Most hosts will be amenable to cooking you something else. We've only been refused outright on one occasion out of dozens of requests we've made for porridge, cereal, or just toast.

If you are on a tighter budget, an interesting lodging option is to stay at one of the universities or colleges in the area you are touring. Many schools rent out rooms during summer vacation time. Many also serve basic student meals to travelers for a very reasonable fee. If you think you might enjoy this somewhat spartan but stimulating type of lodging, write ahead to the British Universities Accommodation Consortium, University Park, Nottingham. They will be happy to send you a list of participating schools and the various particulars. The fees per night tend to be less than £10 per person.

If you are drawn to the amenities of larger hotels, which often have swimming pools and other comforts, there are several hotel chains that operate throughout the U.K. Perhaps the largest is Trusthouse Forte, with an American information office at 12 E 41st Street, New York, NY 10017. Their toll-free number is 800-225–5843. If you anticipate using hotels rather than B&Bs, your travel agent is probably the best source of information, as they will have brochures and books to pore over to pick out the kind of place you want. There is a vast gulf between the top hotels, which go for $200–500 per night in London, $100–200 in the countryside, and the more intimate B&B atmosphere which seldom range above $50 per night for two people.

If you are on a bare-bones budget, youth hostels can be found throughout the U.K. In the U.S., write to the American Youth Hostels, 1332 I Street, N.W., Washington, DC

20005. In the U.K., contact YHA at Trevelyan House, 8 St. Stephen's Hill, St. Albans, Hertfordshire. Both organizations are helpful and enthusiastic supporters of bicycle touring.

The old saying has it that the French live to eat, while the English eat to live. Like many old sayings, there is a grain of truth at the center of it. There is definitely a more utilitarian view of food in the U.K. than on the other side of the Channel. Part of this attitude stems from the venerable British disdain for the sensual, going back to the Victorian era. Then, too, wartime rationing, which lasted well into the 1950s, played a role by giving the British good reason to downplay the function of food as entertainment. However, things are changing. On our last two visits to the U.K., we were pleased to see more and more natural foods restaurants, some with that favorite of ours, the salad bar. Granted, it won't look like that 42-foot salad bar at the Sizzlin' Steak, but it will get you by.

Best of all, the relatively recent waves of immigration from India, Pakistan and the West Indies have given new zip to the British table. The authors happen to love Indian food, so we make a beeline for the curry restaurants as soon as our feet touch British soil. Nowadays, there are many varieties of Indian restaurants to choose among: North, South, Kashmiri, Rajasthani, and other offshoots. One of the best meals we had on a recent visit was at the Sri Lanka restaurant, something we had never sampled before. The curries in the U.K. tend to be on the tame side, so don't be afraid to ask the cook to spice it up. Whatever your taste, you will not have any trouble getting your fill of Indian food. If your taste runs to other directions—Italian, French, or Mexican—you may have to be patient until you get around one of the larger cities.

No matter where you are, you will always be able to find that most ubiquitous of British institutions, the fish and chips shop. Hardly any town will be without one, and they are almost always good, if greasy. The British chip has a taste all its own, quite unlike French *pommes-frites* or American French fries, and can become addictive. As for the fish, there will almost always be a large selection to choose from: plaice, cod, and skate, as well as scallops, oysters, and shrimp. Nowadays, you will also find fried chicken on the menu at many fish and chips shops.

Different regions have their own tasty specialties. For example, even if you think you wouldn't like it, you really have to try haggis when you're up in Scotland. A sort of sausage, haggis tastes better than the sum of its ingredients would have you believe. You can even get it at some Scottish fish and chips shops, deep fried and on a stick. When in Southern England, it is essential to treat yourself to a Devonshire cream tea. Devonshire cream is a thick clotted cream made over a slow fire until it is of a consistency somewhere between butter and sour cream. It is absolutely delicious, spread on a scone with a touch of jam. It is definitely one of those things we think about when we've been away from England for a while.

If you are a cheese lover, you will feast in the English countryside. Of course, most of the well-known French, Italian, and Swiss cheeses are available, but the native products are well worth sampling. Try Wensleydale, with its delicate flavor and slightly sweet aftertaste, or Caerphilly, Leicester (pronounced Lester), and the famous Cheddar. If you are a blue cheese fan, Stilton is widely considered to be the top of the line.

THE PUB SCENE

As we mentioned earlier, the pubs are one place not to miss, even if you are not a big drinker. They are unique gathering spots, each with its own flavor and clientele. Pubs are governed by all sorts of eccentric rules and regulations, closing hours and such. We won't attempt to present all the peculiarities here, but there are a few notable bits of information you should know. Licensing hours, as they are called, vary from place to place, but the general rule is that pubs are open from around 11 A.M. to 3 P.M., then again from around 5 to 11 P.M. These hours can vary a half hour or so from district to district, and on the weekends, so don't quote us as gospel on the subject. Once in a London pub a gentleman with a bowler hat and umbrella tried to explain how it all worked, but either he or we had consumed too much of the local bitter. For whatever reason, it never became totally clear.

Speaking of bitter, this fine beverage is the most popular pub drink. You can get it by the pint (most common) or by the half-pint. Bitter is the name for what in the U.S. would be called draft beer. There will often be other things on tap: lager, hard cider, and usually a darker beverage like Guinness. Guinness can take some getting used to. It is dark, sweet, and rich: all the things we had come not to expect from beer. To top it all off, beer is served at room temperature in the U.K. Don't worry, though, if you like your beer cold. Ask for a cold bottled beer; they will usually have a large variety on display on the bar. But if you want to sound like a local, stride in and ask for a "pint o' the bitter." Each pub will have its own particular brand. Nowadays, many of the pubs are owned by the larger breweries, which will stock the establishment with its own brands, but out in the countryside you can still find the traditional family-owned pub.

One thing to keep your eye on is the bottom line. The price of drinks in Great Britain can vary wildly, and can be exorbitant in the larger cities. More than once, upon seeing the posted prices in a city pub, we've thought, How can these people afford to drink so much? And drink they do: One of our first surprises was noticing how much drinking goes on there. This fact will be particularly noticeable in Ireland, where people reportedly spend a quarter or more of their income on liquor.

Food is available in most pubs. You can almost always get a sandwich, and some pubs have hot food as well. Some of the common pub dishes sound better than they taste, in our humble opinion. There is "bangers and mash," which translates as sausages and mashed potatoes. The British sausage is not known for its high meat content, to say the least, so be prepared for a different-tasting sausage than you might be expecting. Shepherd's pie is widely available, generally consisting of ground beef with a topping of mashed potatoes. There is the famous "bubble and squeak," made with greens and meat, and the cockney delicacy eel pie and mash, just what it sounds like. North Americans may chuckle over the pub dish called "faggots and peas," which is sort of a pork, liver, and onion pie served with a side of peas. The "ploughman's lunch," available just about everywhere, will be a chunk of cheese, some pickles, and a piece of bread. This latter dish, accompanied by a pint of the local bitter, makes a good midday meal for the cyclist. In several pubs on our most recent tour, we noticed that this meal had been renamed the "ploughperson's lunch," in a concession to feminist awareness.

MONEY

The money in the U.K. comes in various denominations of pounds sterling (£). In paper money there are denominations of £1, £5, £10, £20, and £50. In coins, there is also a £1 piece, and 50p, 20p, 10p, 5p, 2p and 1p. Seldom will you hear anyone say "fifty pence"; it will almost always be abbreviated to "fifty p." Sometimes you'll still find the old coins floating around, from before they went to decimal coinage. The shilling is 5p, the two-shilling piece equal to 10p.

The rate of exchange goes up and down every day. Once we were clobbered by a devaluation. At the beginning of a trip our dollar bought a little over two pounds; a few weeks later the dollar slipped and our buying power suffered drastically. On another trip, we got a boost from a change in the exchange rate. The one thing we can guarantee is that you will always lose when you change your money. This varies from a few cents at the bank to sometimes a lot more when you change money at a shop or Bureau de Change (for some reason the French spelling and pronunciation is used in the U.K.).

MAIL

Mail service within the U.K. tends to be better and faster than in the U.S. Postage rates are comparable, costing approximately 50 cents to send a card or light letter back to the U.S.

TELEPHONES

We have had our share of troubles with the eccentric phone system in the British Isles. It is improving with time, but be prepared to treat it delicately, as you would an elderly uncle. First of all, dial the phones or punch the buttons more slowly than you would in the U.S. This helps your hit rate. Second, remember that a ringing telephone in the U.K. sounds somewhat like a busy signal in the U.S. Third, if you are calling from a pay phone, many of them work differently than they do in the U.S. You dial the number, then you hear somebody answer followed by a quick clunk and some beeps. This is your signal to drop your money in. If all goes well the person will then still be on the line to talk to you. On the plus side, there are many telephones available.

One caution to keep in mind: Hotels can tack on pretty much whatever surcharge they want for making phone calls from your room. A recent example: We made a call from our hotel room that we had paid £2 for at a phone booth the day before. When we checked out the charge was £6. Ask before you call, as these surcharges can sometimes be two or three times the cost of your $10 overseas call. We have talked to people who were surprised at checkout with a phone bill for a short call home that equaled the price of their night's lodging. Using your phone credit card's international setup can help you avoid getting stuck with the surcharge.

GENERAL HINTS, TIPS, AND STRATEGIES FOR BICYCLE TOURING

IN THIS CHAPTER WE WILL COVER A NUMBER OF THOSE aspects of bike touring that you might otherwise have to learn the hard way. In fact, that's the way we learned many of the following skills—by making a lot of mistakes. Perhaps you will be able to save yourself time, energy, and sore anatomy by trying out some of this hard-won knowledge.

SAFETY

The most important part of any tour is staying healthy and intact. Europe is probably the safest populated place on earth to ride your bike, but you will still need to keep an eye out for your well-being all the time. It is hard to enter or leave a city any other way than on a crowded thoroughfare, and you will need to use extra caution at these moments. It takes awhile to get used to riding on the left side of the road. Each time we get to the U.K., we forget about it a few times at first, then it becomes second nature. Getting honked at or nearly run over has a quickening effect on the brain's learning curve.

We *always* wear **helmets**, even if we are just going around the block. We urge you to do so, too. You won't see a lot of helmets in Europe, so it may take some extra effort on your part to put it on every day. For our part, we are happy to choose safety over machismo. We have seen too many accidents that could have easily been prevented by simply strapping on a helmet. A friend's father, a vigorous man in the peak of health, nudged a curb a few blocks from his house and took a fall while going probably 2 miles an hour. He hit his head on the sidewalk and died from it instantly. Events like this have inspired us to buy the best helmets we could afford and wear them wherever we go.

The same goes for *eye protection*. We always wear sunglasses, even on short rides. You never know when a stray bug is going to fly your way, so it pays to be prepared. Wraparound glasses or goggles are the way to go, because of increased protection against wind and glare. Wind is hard on eyes: evolution did not foresee that we would be rushing through space against the wind for hours at a time. Glare is a major source of end-of-the-day headaches, so anything you can do to cut it down is to your advantage. Some of the new sunglasses technology is absolutely incredible, much better than anything that was available just a few years ago. We recently upgraded our old goggles to the new wraparound kind, and were amazed at the difference they made.

Mirrors have also come to be important to us. The great advantage of a rearview mirror is that you don't have to keep whipping your head around to see what's coming up behind you. This prevents stiff necks the next morning as well as simply being more efficient. A glance in the mirror takes much less time than craning the neck around, and you run less danger of missteering your bike while looking back. We personally think rearview mirrors are worth their weight in gold, real lifesavers, so we urge you to try them out.

DAILY MAINTENANCE

If you will pay your bike just a few minutes attention each day, it will reward you with hours of service. Neglect those few minutes, however, and look out. Many of the safety problems people have on bike rides come from not noticing little things that need a tiny bit of adjusting. An improperly tightened quick release or a worn brake cable can make a very large difference to your well-being.

Before our first solo tour, we spent an evening at a bike shop learning the fundamentals of bike repair and adjustment. One evening was all that it took to learn enough basics to get by. We carry a couple of miniature repair books with us for minor adjustments (one of the best is Rob Van Der Plas's *Roadside Bicycle Repairs*, published by Kampman; $3.95). Anything more complicated goes to a bike shop. Before riding each day, we always make the following quick checks:

Quick releases: We make sure they are tightened down properly, having learned the hard way that bicycle gremlins can loosen these gadgets while you sleep.

Tire pressure: A squeeze will tell you whether you have the right amount of air in your tire. Keeping tires inflated to their right amount will prevent such common problems as pinched (snake-bit) tubes, as well as keeping you rolling down the road most efficiently.

Brakes: We take a look at the cable to make sure it's still in good shape, then squeeze the brakes a few times to be sure they are grabbing. When bikes come out of the hands of the airlines, the brakes always seem to need a little adjusting. During a tour, brakes seem to need attention every couple of days.

Chains: Keep them lubricated. A tube of Tri-Flow has accompanied us all over the world. There are probably other excellent products that do the same thing, but this is the one we always use. A drop on each chain link does it, and should be repeated every few days on a long tour. When your chain gets shiny, it's time for more. We change chains about once a year, more often if it has been a heavy travel year.

Handlebars: Give them a twist in all the relevant directions before you start each day. After having the unsettling but attention-focusing experience of having handlebars come off in our hands a couple of times, we give them a heroic pull up, down and sideways before riding off.

Derailleurs: We like to shift our gears up and down a few times in the first few minutes of a ride to be sure they are functioning smoothly. Adjustment of derailleurs is one of the facts of life in the saddle, so you might as well do it early in the day.

Seat height and angle: Once you get your seat at the right height and angle you probably will not have to bother with it again. It is worth checking it each day, however, because many sore knees, shoulders, and numb crotches are the result of improper seat adjustment. Get a good bike shop to show you just how to position your seat and its angle to give you the most efficient and comfortable stroke.

WARMING UP

We have found that our touring day goes much more smoothly if we take a few minutes to stretch before riding, and then take it easy the first mile or two. Warming up is sometimes hard to remember because you will often be excited about setting off on the day's ride. It has been our experience that many of the common complaints, such as achy knees at the end of the day, are the result of starting off too quickly and without a warm-up. The joints of the body contain material that is designed to cushion shock and friction, but to do so efficiently it must be warm. The reason is that the material expands when it is warm, and it is the expansion which gives it its cushioning power. Just as your pillow needs fluffing in the morning after being slept on overnight, your joints need some "fluffing" to get the night's flatness and stiffness out of them. The following stretches will warm your joints slowly and gently. Your first few minutes on the bike should also be slow and gentle. We make it a practice to ride around five or ten minutes first if we have to tackle a big hill first thing in the morning. The older you are, the more important your warm-up is. Both of us are in our forties, but since learning to stretch and warm up properly we have never missed a day's touring because of soreness or injury. Here are the four easy stretches that we have evolved over the years. We are by no means experts on stretching; these exercises are simply those which have worked for us. If you would like a more formal series of bike stretches, read Bob Anderson's thorough book on the subject, *Stretching* (Shelter Publication; $9.95).

Stretch No. 1: Lie on your back on the floor. Bring your knees up and clasp your arms around them. Breathe deeply and slowly as you rock gently around, massaging your lower back. Keep your stomach muscles relaxed; induce the rocking motion with your hands. Continue for a minute or two, until the low back and sacral area feel warmed up, then stretch out and relax for a little while.

Stretch No. 2: Sit on the floor with your legs stretched out in front of you. Place your hands on your thighs. As you breathe out slowly, lean forward and slide your hands down your legs as far as is comfortable for you. As you breathe in, slide your hands back up your legs. Repeat for a minute or two, in coordination with your breathing. Each time you slide down your legs with your hands, you may notice you go a little farther.

Stretch No. 3: Lie on your stomach, propping yourself up on your elbows. Breathing slowly and deeply, raise each leg in turn 3 or 4 inches off the floor. Do these lifts slowly and gently, raising the legs just a few inches and then lowering them.

Stretch No. 4: Take your right hand and grip your left shoulder. Breathing slowly and deeply, turn your head gently from side to side. Turn first toward the side you are holding, then

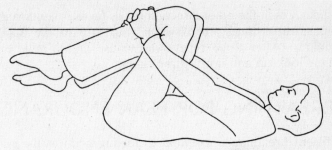

STRETCH NO. 1

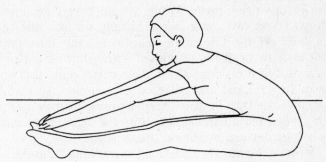

STRETCH NO. 2

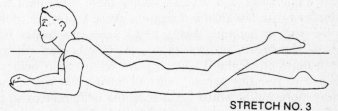

STRETCH NO. 3

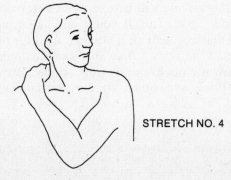

STRETCH NO. 4

180 degrees in the other direction (or as far as is comfortable). Repeat three times, then switch your grip to the opposite shoulder. After three repetitions, pause in the middle and slowly look up and down three times.

BREATHING FOR PEAK ENDURANCE

Efficient breathing is essential to feeling good at the end of the touring day. Nature has handed us an obstacle to overcome in this department. When human beings get upset or undergo stress, we move our breathing up into our chests. This fires off the adrenaline machinery, the three-million-year-old fight or flight response. Adrenaline is a powerful stimulant, but it is designed for short bursts only. It is important to stay relaxed and centered as you ride, so that your breathing can stay in your deep abdomen as well as your chest. When the breathing is only in the chest, the heart has to work harder and the blood pressure goes up.

Most of the blood circulation in your lungs is in the lower third, between the bottom of your sternum and your navel. Over a quart of blood circulates down there every minute, as compared with less than a teacup up at the top of your lungs, below your collarbone. Many of us keep our bellies tight, forcing the breath up into the chest. Our bodies will work much more efficiently if we can learn to relax our bellies. If we had to give one general piece of advice that would make riding more fun, it would be to keep the belly relaxed so that you can breathe deeply down into your abdomen as well as up in your chest. That way, you will be using all the territory that nature has provided inside you. If you would like a tape that details efficient breathing activities, you can send for one that Gay has recorded (*The Art of Breathing and Centering*, available from your favorite bookstore or from Audio Renaissance, 5858 Wilshire Boulevard, Suite 205, Los Angeles, CA 90036; $9.95).

WHAT TO TAKE

It ought to go without saying that, in the realm of what to take, less is better. We have got our traveling act pretty well pared down by now, and will be happy to share our insights. It is our practice to take no more than our panniers and one fanny pack will carry. If you shop for panniers carefully, you can find ones that also may be carried onto an airplane rather than checked through. This will keep you from the hazards of lost baggage. Pannier technology has changed enormously for the better over the past few years, and is getting better all the time. Whatever we could tell you would be out of date by the time you go shopping, except for a few general guidelines. Our suggestion is to get panniers that attach and detach easily, are light, tough, washable, and are a snap to pack and repack. Waterproof material is an obvious requirement. Panniers tend to be quite expensive as such things go, but if possible, get the very best you can.

Here is a list of what we took on a tour not long ago.

helmet
gloves, both fingerless riding gloves and light leather gloves
Gore-tex jacket and pants
riding shorts with reinforced seats (2 pairs)
T-shirts (3)
socks (3 pairs)
thermal silk underwear
riding shoes
toiletries
first-aid kit
tool kit, lubricant, 2 spare tubes
bathing suits (2)
sunscreen, lip cream
paperback books (I each)
camera (I each)
sunglasses and goggles

The following articles were also carried for fancy restaurants, city visits, and other occasions when we needed to dress up a little.

trousers (2 pairs)
sweaters (1 each)
underwear
(Kathlyn) 2 silk evening outfits—slacks, top, jacket
    stockings (2 pairs)
    dress shoes (1 pair)
(Gay) sport coat
    tie
    dress shoes (1 pair)

In addition, we each had a small fanny pack to carry whatever we wanted easiest access to: map, camera, sunscreen—items like these are best carried within easy reach.

The weight of all these items came to just under ten pounds each, not bad at all for a couple of weeks in a foreign country. The silk really helps keep the weight of clothing down. It's surprising how much a couple of dresses or slacks can add to the space and the weight, so if you need to take fancier outfits you might be on the lookout for silk items. It gets wrinkled, but we have a tiny lightweight steamer that works wonders on it in just a couple of minutes.

PART TWO

THE TOURS

THE KEYS

Two standard keys will be used throughout the tours. The first is a key to the difficulty of the terrain on specific days. The three levels of difficulty are Easy, Moderate, and Challenging. *Easy* terrain is largely flat. There may be hills, but they will tend to be of the sort that do not require you to stand up on the pedals. *Moderate* terrain has a significantly greater number of hills than Easy. *Challenging* terrain means that the climbs are steep or long, sometimes requiring that you dismount and walk or at least stand up on the pedals for a significant stretch. Some days will be marked with a combination, such as Moderate to Challenging. Obviously any sort of keying is subjective: the levels of difficulty are assessed by two fortyish riders who are in shape but not athletes by any means.

The second key is to price in lodging and restaurants; the three categories are Modest, Medium, and Top. *Modest* refers to lodgings or dinner for two (with one drink apiece) for the equivalent of less than $50. *Medium* refers to lodgings or dinner for $50–100. *Top* refers to lodgings or dinner for over $100. Times may change, and events such as devaluation may occur to your favor or not, so please take our key in the spirit in which it was intended: helpful but not carved in stone.

If the price key is not noted, this means that cost is in the Modest range.

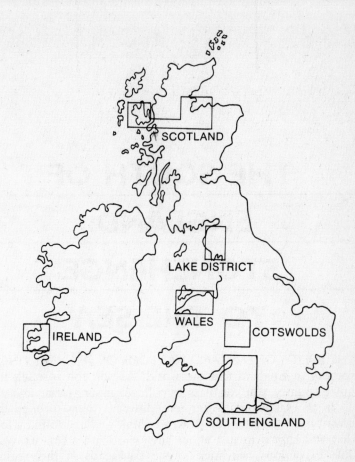

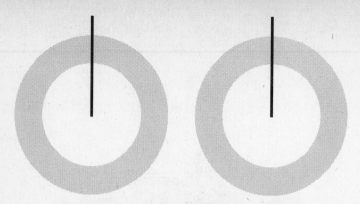

THE SOUTH OF ENGLAND: STONEHENGE TO THE SEA

THE SOUTH OF ENGLAND HAS SOME OF THE VERY FINEST scenery in England and the world. As you roll through this quiet country you can pass by village, moor, farm, and sea all in the same day. After four different tours through this countryside since the late '70s, we think we have found a tour that will appeal to just about anybody. With a few unavoidable exceptions, we stick to the backroads in this region, where much of the magnificence is to be found. We begin the tour in Avon and Wiltshire, then ride through Dorset and a small piece of Devon, finally turning north again to end the tour in the Somerset town of Glastonbury.

This area is one of the last places where the Old Country still flourishes. When you are riding through this green countryside, it is easy to forget that you are only an hour or so from London by train. You won't see nearly as many smiling faces in London as you will in the countryside. Here a stop in a pub will get you a welcome from both the innkeeper and the locals enjoying their pints. Buy them a round and you'll have a hard time getting away when it's time for you to go. Antiquities are everywhere. The greatest prehistoric monuments of our ancestors are on view at Stonehenge and Avebury, along with castles, and ancient churches and abbeys. But you may feel, as we have come to, that the real treasure here is the land itself and its caretakers.

STARTING THE TOUR

We start this tour in Bath for two reason. First, Bath is a fascinating place to visit for its own sake, and second, it is easy to get to from London. Here's how you get to Bath by rail, assuming you come to the U.K. by air. If you arrive at Heathrow, take the Underground to Earl's Court and change for Paddington Station. From Paddington, trains run every hour or so to Bath. From Gatwick, take the trains that run to Victoria Station, then transfer to Paddington by the Underground. You can take your bike on the Underground during off-peak hours, that is, not during rush hours. If you absolutely have to get to London during rush hour, you might be able to get a cabbie to take your gear and you aboard, although some are reluctant to do this.

WHERE TO STAY AND DINE IN BATH

One of the most pleasant places we found around Bath was the Fern Cottage Hotel, set in an eighteenth-century house with gardens in the nearby village of Batheaston (9 Northend, Batheaston, Bath; tel. [0225]858190. (Medium, with breakfast)

Two smaller B&Bs are Sovereign House (38 St. James Park, Bath; tel. [0225]338162) and the Albany Guest House (21 Crescent Gardens, Bath; tel [0225]313339). Both are clean and staffed by friendly hosts. (both Modest)

To sink yourself in the eighteenth-century feel of Bath, you might choose the elegant Royal Crescent Hotel (16 Royal Crescent, Bath BA1 2LS; tel. [0225]319090). You'll experience sumptuous surroundings, a top-of-the-line restaurant, and the heart of Bath's cosmopolitan appeal. (Top)

Many people think Bath is where some of England's finest food is to be found. If your taste runs to light, nouvelle cuisine, try out Tarts (tel. [0225]330280), which is innovative enough to justify the cost. Reservations are probably necessary for their small dining room. (Medium–Top)

There is also a good Japanese restaurant here, a rarity in England. It's called Chikako's (tel. [0225]664125). (Medium) There are also several Indian restaurants, as well as dozens of other options.

WHAT TO DO IN BATH

The big attraction in Bath is the Baths. You can tour the restored remains of an elaborate and large public bath built by those luxury-loving former residents, the Romans. Actually, the Romans had trouble with rheumatism; their warm Mediterranean climate did not prepare them for the rigors of clammy England. Connected to the Baths is The Pump Room (tel. [0225]461111, ext. 327), where you can sip tea while listening to live chamber music. You can also sample the mineral waters, which taste horrible. There is also a fine theater in Bath that often has recent hits from the London stage. In fact, Bath has such a blend of beautiful architecture, cultural opportunities, and many historical buildings, that you may want to spend a day biking and strolling the side streets and avenues before continuing on the tour.

DAY ONE: BATH TO AVEBURY

(39 miles; easy to moderate)
Today's destination is the remarkable prehistoric monument of Avebury. Many people think that Avebury is a more impressive sight even than Stonehenge, and we are inclined to agree. Avebury is laid out across a much larger territory than

Stonehenge. Then, too, the stones at Avebury are integrated into the modern village, making for a marked contrast. In addition, you can walk among the stones, while at Stonehenge you must view them from behind a fence. This is understandable, of course; people were causing damage to the monument. But at Avebury, it is possible to sit right next to a druid holy monument and meditate on the grandeur of it all. In today's 39-mile ride you'll encounter easy and moderately hilly sections of roads, a good introduction to this moderate to challenging tour. Pack a picnic lunch from Bath's food shops, to enjoy at your stop in Castle Combe or an idyllic spot of your choosing.

We begin the tour in front of the railroad station.

Leave Bath on the main road to Chippenham, the A4. You won't be on the main road long, and it happens to be the easiest way out of town. The road is wide enough for cycling; in fact, last time we were there we shared the road with a team of about a dozen racing cyclists as we rode out of town.

(*Note:* Many of the English back roads are poorly marked or in some cases not marked at all. This can be frustrating at times. We have done our best to give clear directions, but we ourselves got lost a few times. As any veteran cycle tourist will tell you, getting lost is half the fun. In this part of the world, however, it is not possible to get very lost. Southern England is quite densely populated, so, if you miss one of our twists and turns, just ask a native.)

At the stop light, continue on the A4. (sign: Chippenham) You'll see the beginnings of rolling hills to your right with clusters of farmhouses on the ridges. The road rises into **Batheaston.**

Turn left at a road marked Northend, St. Catherine. There is an immediate steep climb here, then you'll roll downhill on this narrow road. You pass between stone houses covered with ivy, up and down little hills.

At the Y fork quite soon, go right toward St. Catherine. The road now emerges into fields lined with walls and hedges—pristine English countryside.

Less than a mile later, turn right at a Y fork. (sign: Colerne) This one-lane road is made for cycling. The road goes up and down gentle hills for a mile or two.

When you come to an unmarked T, turn right onto a level road with fields on the left, trees on the right.

Less than a block later, turn left at another T.

Then immediately turn right, following the signs toward Colerne and Castle Combe. Continue along this road, passing through field and forest.

A few miles later, you come to a T intersection, where you will turn right on 420.

Immediately turn left onto the Castle Combe road, not marked by a number. After a climb of about a mile the road levels out, passing through views of rolling hills, fields, and forest.

Take the Y fork toward Castle Combe. Shortly you come into **Castle Combe,** one of this region's "must-see" villages. A few years ago, Castle Combe was voted England's prettiest village. It is a living treasure of architecture, with not a stone or a rose out of place.

Leave Castle Combe by turning right on B4039. (sign: Chippenham)

Keep following the signs for Chippenham at the next couple of intersections.

After 2 miles or so junction onto A420 toward Chippenham. A bike path will appear on your left. This stretch of road can be busy. Stay on it all the way into **Chippenham,** a distance of a mile or so.

Leave Chippenham, taking A4059 toward Lyncham The road winds uphill through a residential area then on out of town, becoming A4069.

A mile later, turn right toward Langley Burrell and East Tytherton.

Follow the signs to E. Tytherton, through a stone tunnel and over a stone bridge. There is a lovely old church here with leaded windows, and the occasional farmhouse in the distance. The road is smooth and even all the way into the village of **East Tytherton.**

Take a left toward Foxham and Charlcutt.

A mile later, turn right toward Charlcutt. The road narrows to a lane here and heads uphill quite steeply for ¼ mile.

Turn left toward Hilmarton. You will see the thatched roofs and modern houses of **Spirthull,** with a great view of the valley you've just left. Cruise downhill through open fields and veer right, then uphill again for about a mile.

Turn right toward Hilmarton at the top of this moderate hill. You'll pedal downhill through trees and hedgerows for approximately a mile.

Turn left on A3102. (sign: Lyneham) Climbing once again, you pass the sign Goatacre. Stay on the main road.

Turn right after 3 miles at the signs to Preston and Bushton. This bumpier road leaves the city and moves into rural land again after a mile or so. Farms and fields line the mostly flat road.

Take a right at the sign to Clyffe Pypard.

At the X intersection go straight across, following the sign to
Clyffe Pypard. The Trotting House on the right may be open
if you want a snack. After a couple of miles you roll into
Clyffe Pypard.

Head right at the sign to Broad Hinton. The road climbs steeply
here through a glorious forest for about ¼ mile. At the summit, go left, following the signs to Broad Hinton, where the
land opens up into broad fields and rows of windbreak trees.

After just a mile, take a left toward Broad Hinton. Your route
here has gentle up and downhills through the broad fields.

Turn right after another mile into the town of **Broad Hinton.**

Go right on A361. (sign: Avebury) For your remaining 4½
miles you will roll over small hills in more open pastureland.
You'll see the main attraction, large stones across several
hills, as you pedal into the town of **Avebury.**

At Avebury you can walk up to and touch the stones.
Avebury henge is actually quite large in its entirety, twenty-
eight acres surrounded by an outer bank a mile in circumfer-
ence that originally stood 55 feet high. Only twenty-seven of
the estimated one hundred original stones remain, and they
are magnificent, even daunting. The larger circle originally
surrounded smaller circles that may have contributed to the
building of the village. Many of the stones were eradicated
several hundred years ago. In fact, the ones you can view
today are standing largely because they were buried as hea-
then monuments in the fourteenth century.

WHERE TO STAY AND DINE IN AVEBURY

The village houses several shops with local crafts, and a fine
little tea shop, Stones, where we dined on fresh potato salad,
a hearty mushroom and vegetable soup, and scones with thick
clotted cream. This is the best food opportunity in the area,
and you need to reach there before 6 P.M., when it closes. A
tourist information shop can assist you with accommodations

until 5 P.M. There are several B&Bs in the Modest range near Avebury. Mrs. Jane Lees runs Hollis Cottage (tel. [06723]200), an eighteenth century cottage very near the stone circles. St. Andrews Cottage, also near the monuments, is run by Mrs. Peak-Garland (tel. [06723]247).

DAILY SUMMARY

SOUTH OF ENGLAND TOUR

Day One: Bath to Avebury

(39 miles; easy to moderate)

- Start on the main road to Chippenham, the A4.
- At the stop light, continue on the A4 (sign: Chippenham).
- After a mile or so you come to Batheaston.
- Go left at a road marked Northend, St. Catherine.
- In less than a mile, go right at the fork (sign: Colerne).
- After less than 2 miles, turn right at the unmarked T onto a level road with field on the left, trees on the right.
- Less than one block later, go left at another T.
- Immediately turn right (signs: Colerne, Castle Combe).
- After a few miles, take a right at the T intersection onto 420.
- Turn left immediately onto the Castle Combe road (no number).
- Take the Y fork into Castle Combe.
- Leave Castle Combe on the B4039 right (sign: Chippenham.)
- Keep following the signs for Chippenham at the next couple of intersections.
- After about 2 miles, turn onto A410 toward Chippenham, which appears in a mile or so.
- Take the A4059 toward Lyncham, which becomes A4069.
- After a mile, turn right toward Langley Burrel and East Tytherton.
- Follow the signs to E. Tytherton.
- In East Tytherton, turn left toward Foxham and Charlcutt.
- After a mile, go right toward Charlcutt.
- In ¼ mile, go left toward Hilmarton.
- Passing through Spirthull, turn right toward Hilmarton after a mile.
- After another mile, turn left on A3102 (sign: Lyncham).

- Head right after 3 miles (signs: Preston, Bushton).
- After a little over a mile, take a right (sign: Clyffe Pypard).
- Go straight across at the X intersection (sign: Clyffe Pypard).
- Riding through Clyffe Pypard after 2 miles, head right (sign: Broad Hinton).
- Follow signs over the next couple of miles to Broad Hinton.
- In Broad Hinton, turn right on A361 (sign: Avebury).
- 4½ miles on A361 takes you into Avebury.

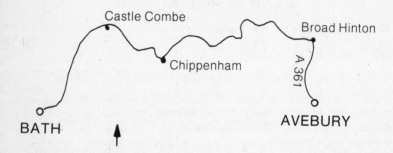

DAY TWO: AVEBURY TO SALISBURY

(30 miles; moderate)
Some people say that Avebury is a more compelling sight than Stonehenge. Today you'll have the opportunity to decide because you will begin the day among the stones at Avebury, then cruise past Stonehenge, ending in Salisbury. The road that most people take down to Stonehenge is very crowded. The route we have devised for today follows scenic back roads for most of its approximately 30 miles. There is really no outstanding lunch stop for today. We recommend packing a picnic and taking tea where you fancy.

You'll leave Avebury on the A362 leading toward Devizes. The slight hills take you quickly to two other Druid monuments, Silbury Hill and the Long Barrow.

To get to these, go left, after ½ **mile, at the roundabout on A4.** (sign: Marlborough) On your left you'll see Silbury Hill.

Why did our rock-loving ancestors build this huge, 130-foot
high mound of dirt? Nobody knows. There are several theo-
ries: the burial ground of a king, an ancient sundial, a sea-
sonal form of the goddess, among others. We do know that
it took a huge number of people with shovels to create this
wondrous hill in about 2500 B.C. The West Kennet Long Barrow, a striking Neolithic burial chamber, is just along here,
too. There are markers which will tell you some of the specu-
lations about these unusual creations.

In about 2 miles you come into **West Kennet.**

Here you take the right road. (signs: E. Kennet, Woodborough) The road follows a small stream into the redbrick
houses in the village of **East Kennet.** You exit this small village riding up a ½-mile hill, then down to the T junction.

Turn right on an easy uphill grade past curving, manicured hills.
(sign: Woodborough) The pavement turns to the right and
curves past the lovely Vale of Pewsey, famous for its white
horse inscribed in the chalk of the hillside (apparently a long-
standing custom in this area), down into **Alton Priors.** Another mile takes you into the larger town of **Woodborough,**
whose homes are spread out through the fields.

Go straight toward Alcott and follow the main road past a
couple of well-maintained thatch-roofed houses and the village
of **Hilcott.** Out of town the route rises a little, then descends
through hedgerows and levels out after 3 miles in **North
Newton.**

At the roundabout, go on A345 toward Salisbury and Upavon.
The trees are taller here and with the hedges shade the road
pleasantly as you pedal along. About 10 miles from West Kennet, you come into **Upavon,** which has many beautiful houses
with thatched roofs.

At the T intersection, take a right, then an immediate left to
stay on the A345. This rises on a slight upgrade through more
great bicycling territory—fields and stands of trees. Another

2 miles brings you into **West Chisenbury,** then with another mile into **Enford.**

This village has several whitewashed, thatch-roofed cottages along the road that follows the Kennet and Avon Canal. You continue on an uphill grade with larger areas of trees clustered around the stream and the small hamlet of Neveravon to your right.

A couple of miles out of town, continue on the road toward Amesbury. Ride up a hill with a military base on your left. Cresting the hill you'll see the houses of Figheldean in the valley to your left. Continuing for 1½ miles brings you to another moderate hill, leveling out into pastureland that had the sweet smell of fresh hay on the breeze the day we passed through. **Durrington** is situated among rolling hills about 2 miles from your last intersection.

Take the right road toward Larkhill at the roundabout. A mile into this road you'll see the Salisbury Plain through the trees to your left. You'll pedal up through the stores and houses of the military base here, then through a series of moderate hills over open plains and a military installation.

After 2 miles or so take the left road here toward Salisbury. The route here for a mile leans into one long downhill and a short climb.

Turn left on A344. (sign: Amesbury) Now you will catch sight of that astounding collection of stones that has been drawing people for millennia. Stonehenge is everything its reputation says it is, partly because of its location on the plain. Every time we've been to Stonehenge the Salisbury Plain has been dappled in ever-changing light.

After admiring the powerful site, which closes its direct access at 6 P.M., turn right on A360. (sign: Salisbury) Ride back up the hill and over the Salisbury Plain, where, we can say from direct experience, the wind can blow heartily at times, challenging your forward momentum.

Go left on A360 after 2 miles. (sign: Salisbury) The path rises and falls through several small hills.

At this roundabout stay on A360. (sign: Salisbury) This route covers more hilly country and one large ring of trees. You'll encounter one steep hill in this section, of about ¼ mile.

About 4 miles down this road, go left. (sign: The Woodfords) You get a thrilling downhill run here through fields of sheep and the tidy little houses of **Middle Woodford.**

Go right at the signs for Lower Woodford and Salisbury. The Avon flows to your left in this gorgeous riverbank valley. One splendid thatch-roofed, redbrick house follows another. Just out of town the road rises slightly, leading you in 1½ miles to the next intersection.

Follow the signs to Salisbury, after which the road levels out.

Go right toward Salisbury after a little bridge. You'll ride through the residential area of **Old Sarum,** original site of the bishop's see and a good place to overlook the city, as the population density rises sharply. Red brick is the building material of choice here.

Turn right onto Castle Road at the roundabout.

Follow the signs to City Center. The spire of the cathedral ahead will help orient you in this big city.

WHERE TO STAY AND DINE IN SALISBURY

This is quite a large town, with a great many sleeping and dining options. The New Inn (43 New Street, Salisbury, SP1 2PH; tel. [0722]27679) is one of the best, although it tends to book up well in advance. There is no smoking allowed at the inn. This inn is housed in a fifteenth-century building. (Medium)

The Grasmere (70 Harnham Road, Salisbury SP2 8JN; tel. [0722]338388) only has five bedrooms, but fine ones they are, mostly with views looking out toward the cathedral. It is a Victorian-style house with an acre or so of grounds around it. (Medium)

Many people think the best meal in town is at Crustaceans (tel. [0722]333948), and, if you like fish, you may agree. The menu offers a wide variety of seafood with both standard and ingenious preparations. (Medium)

Although we tend to steer clear of "English" cuisine, we found that the Haunch of Venison (tel. [0722]22024) had enough innovative flair to recommend it. You actually can get a haunch of venison here, as well as wild game dishes and more traditional fare, such as roast beef and Yorkshire pudding. Salisbury has an array of Indian restaurants and a couple of Chinese ones.

WHAT TO SEE AND DO IN SALISBURY

Salisbury Cathedral is one of the most magnificent in England. It is also unusual in its having been planned and executed in only thirty-eight years (in the fourteenth century). It's not surprising that a city easily grew up around this central focus, whose spire would be an engineering feat in any century. Besides the fine stonework and windows, you can view the original Magna Carta here. What we most enjoyed in this favorite of English cathedrals is its palpable sense of serenity and tranquillity.

On the secular side, you'll enjoy ambling through the town center, which features large and small shops catering to your every need, from fine chocolates to typewriter ribbons. Salisbury is a combination of cultural center and market town, and on the open-air market day when we passed through, the square had a festive, convivial feel that is sometimes outweighed by more modern shopping styles.

DAILY SUMMARY

SOUTH OF ENGLAND TOUR

Day Two: Avebury to Salisbury

(30 miles; moderate)

- Exit Avebury on A362 (sign: Devizes).
- After ½ mile, turn left at the roundabout on A4 (sign: Marlborough).
- Passing Silbury Hill and the West Kennet Long Barrow, go right in West Kennet (sign: E. Kennet, Woodborough).
- After less than a mile, turn right at the T junction (sign: Woodborough).
- Pass through Alton Priors and into Woodborough.
- Go straight here toward Alcott and follow the main road into Hilcott.
- You'll reach North Newton in 3 miles, where you take A345 at the roundabout (signs: Salisbury, Upavon).
- In Upavon, which is 10 miles from West Kennet, turn right, then immediately left to remain on the A345.
- In 2 miles you'll ride through West Chisenbury.
- Another mile passes through Enford.
- 2 miles from this town, continue on the road toward Amesbury.
- Durrington is approximately 2 miles from this intersection.
- Turn right at the roundabout (sign: Larkhill).
- In 2 miles take the left road toward Salisbury.
- After about 1 mile, go left on A344 (sign: Amesbury), which takes you to Stonehenge.
- After your visit, turn right on A360 (sign: Salisbury).
- Go left on A360 after 2 miles (sign: Salisbury).
- Stay on A360 at the next roundabout.
- After about 4 miles, go left (sign: The Woodfords), which goes through Middle Woodford.
- Go right at the signs for Lower Woodford and Salisbury.
- After 1½ miles, follow the sign to Salisbury at this intersection.
- Go right toward Salisbury after a little bridge.
- Old Sarum is on the outskirts of Salisbury.
- Turn right on Castle Road at the roundabout.
- Follow the signs to the City Center of Salisbury.

AVEBURY

Vale of Pewsey

Upavon

A 345

Stonehenge

A 360

SALISBURY

DAY THREE: SALISBURY TO BLANDFORD FORUM

(25 miles; moderate)
Today you will cruise through fields and villages on an excursion to a perfect English town. Except for the first couple of miles, this day's approximately 25 mile ride is along little-trafficked back roads and is only moderately hilly.

Leave Salisbury on the A354. (sign: Blandford Forum) This road winds through the suburbs of Salisbury on small hills, then takes you on a longer incline through a canopy of trees.

After 2 miles you come into **Coombe Bissett.** Stay on the main road through this pretty village. A moderate hill leads out of town past sheep pastures on the surrounding hills. After a 2-mile incline, you'll see a sign directing you to turn left toward Rockbourne.

Turn left up the hill. (sign: Rockbourne)

Bend around toward Rockbourne after about a mile. The road here is fairly level for a little-traveled stretch of open fields and hills to your right. Soon you'll come into **Rockbourne,** which has a profusion of thatched roofs and flower-bedecked walls.

Just outside Rockbourne, turn right. (signs: Damerham, Cranborne) The road narrows and inclines upward under overhanging trees for about a ½ mile, then winds downhill to the next junction.

Go right at the junction. (sign: Martin)

Go right again shortly. (signs: Martin, Cranborne)

After about 100 yards, turn left. (sign: Cranborne) This little road is the essence of rural England: narrow, hedge-lined, with open fields as far as the eye can see.

Turn left between berry bush–lined hedges, toward Fordingbridge. After ¼ of a mile, you will come to the village of **Damerham.**

Continue on the road to Fordingbridge, the B3078. Just after your turn is an exquisite manor house on your left. You then enter another tree-shaded canopy on a slight uphill. The rich, loamy smell of fertile farmland was particularly heavy on the morning air when we last visited. It was also right along here that we passed an elderly gentleman riding a tandem bicycle all by himself. You enter **Fordingbridge** three miles after leaving Damerham.

You may want to stop for a stretch here in this pleasant redbrick town before moving on. It's a surprisingly busy little place, with a thirteenth-century church.

Turn right at the sign to Alderholt and Cranborne. In 2 miles you pass through **Alderholt,** where you follow the signs to Cranborne. The road quickly becomes hedge-lined again as you ride on a slight upgrade out into the fields. There are several small junctions: keep following the road to Cranborne. Along here, just before you crest a hill, a thatched cottage houses local pottery. Afterward, descend into wilder country than the manicured scenery we have passed so far today. You'll come into the lovely village of **Cranborne** 6½ miles after leaving Alderholt.

Take a left at the sign for Winborne Minster.

At two quick junctions take the direction toward Winborne Minster.

About a mile later, continue straight across the intersection. (signs: Winborne, B3078) A series of modest hills takes you past occasional farmhouses and lots of open, rolling fields. Continue along the main road with signs to Winborne. This section of the ride is interspersed with wooded copses off in the distance. Soon you will pass a series of picturesque cottages, one of which has leaded windows and an unusual sloping roof. You'll climb a couple of short hills before coming into **Winborne Minster.**

This is a good-sized town with a church and a pleasant feel to it. It is a good place to stop for tea before riding on to Blandford. Winborne market is one of the largest open and covered markets in the area, and has a fascinating flea market on Saturday mornings. An English flea market holds an amazing array of eccentric merchandise for sale. These markets are invariably crowded, so you might want to go early before people get cleaned out of their antique pickle jars and the like. If you take time to walk around this town, you may find the gem of a garden in the Priest's House Museum and Garden on the busy High Street.

Staying on the B3082 leave town toward Tarrant Keyneston.
The road has gentle up and down slopes as you enter a length of tall tree canopy that continues for quite a while. A little way into the canopied stretch you will see a sign directing you to the Badbury Rings. These large concentric mounds of earth surrounding a stand of trees were ancient burial grounds and the center of an early road network. After visiting the Rings, head on through the trees. Descending a hill, you pass through the small village of **Tarrant Keyneston**.

The road continues to crest and dip through the smooth fields. An enviably placed golf course appears on your right, then you top a final hill and slope down into the famous town of **Blandford Forum,** the end of today's tour.

WHERE TO STAY AND DINE IN BLANDFORD FORUM

Blandford is a pretty crossroads town that is large enough to have plenty of amenities but not so big as to lose the backroads feel of this tour. We enjoyed strolling around the tree-lined streets of town and shopping in the Safeway.

The tourist information stand is near the Safeway, and the people there were extremely cordial when we visited them.

If you are in the mood for good living and eating, La Belle Alliance (tel. [0258]452842) is an elegant country restaurant and small hotel in a near-downtown setting. It only has five bedrooms, so a call ahead is probably in order. (Medium)

If you would like a farmhouse B&B out of town, we can recommend one run by Mr. and Mrs. Tory. Get the directions at the tourist information bureau or call the owners at [0258]452919. (Modest)

If you pause here long enough to get to know the area, you'll find that Blandford has some interesting places to visit. For example, Milton Abbas is one of the finest examples to be found of a model thatch-roofed village. Also, Kingston

Lacy is a house and grounds in the grand tradition near Badbury Rings.

DAILY SUMMARY

SOUTH OF ENGLAND TOUR

Day Three: Salisbury to Blandford Forum

(25 miles; moderate)

- Leave Salisbury on the A354 (sign: Blandford Forum).
- Stay on the main road 2 miles into Coombe Bissett and for 2 miles after this village.
- Turn left up the hill here (sign: Rockbourne).
- Head toward Rockbourne about a mile.
- Just outside Rockbourne, turn right (signs: Damerham, Cranborne).
- Turn right after less than a mile at the junction (sign: Martin).
- Go right again very shortly (signs: Martin, Cranborne).
- Turn left after about 100 yards (sign: Cranborne).
- Turn left toward Fordingbridge.
- After ¼ mile, in Damerham, continue on the B3078 (sign: Fordingbridge).
- You'll come into Fordingbridge after 3 miles.
- Go right at the sign to Alderhot and Cranborne.
- After 2 miles, in Alderholt, follow the signs to Cranborne.
- Turn left at the sign for Winborne Minster.
- At two successive junctions, take the direction toward Winborne Minster.
- After a mile, continue straight across the intersection (sign: Winborne, B3078).
- Stay on the B3082 in Winborne, about 9½ miles from Cranborne.
- Pass the Badbury Rings and Tarrant Keyneston.
- The B3082 goes all the way into Blandford Forum.

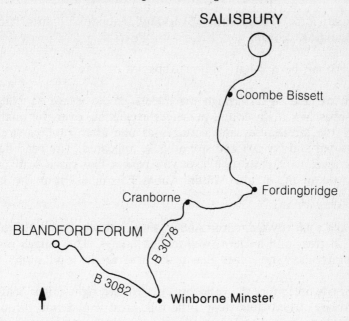

DAY FOUR: BLANDFORD FORUM TO ABBOTSBURY

(45–47 miles; moderate)
Today's longer, 45–47 mile journey will take you through fine English countryside to end in a village that still has the feel of the Middle Ages.

Leave Blandford on the A354. (sign: Dorchester)

Shortly thereafter, go right at the next junction. In a little ways you will see a sign directing you to Winterborne Strickland.

Take this little road through high hedges. The climb is fairly steep for the first mile. Believe it or not, there is glorious scenery visible on the other side of the hedgerow. After about 3½ miles a deep mossy woods appears on your right. You turn and roll downhill through sparkling farmland on this back road into **Winterborne Strickland,** about 5 miles from Blandford Forum.

Turn left here. (sign: Milton Abbas)

Follow the signs through the middle of the village to Milton Abbas. We really found ourselves exclaiming over the quality of the farmhouses and cottages as one after another slope-roofed and ivy-covered stone house appeared. The road here is level to slightly uphill as you pass a low stone wall and cattle in the fields. **Milton Abbas** (2½ miles from the last junction).

Take a left toward Milton Abbey. You go down the hill through lush trees and ancient, well-tended homes. This village is an immaculate showplace that really deserves its reputation.

At the bottom of the residential street, turn right. (sign: Milton Abbey) Climb this steep little hill, crest it and ride through the little tunnel and down to visit the abbey. There has been a church on this beautiful site for the past millennium; now the abbey doubles as an exclusive boarding school. Be sure to visit the fifteenth-century hanging tabernacle. The surrounding grounds with their regally arching trees are perfect for resting the eyes and legs.

After leaving the abbey grounds, turn right to return to Milton Abbas. Your previous downhill becomes a brief climb before descending to the main road.

Turn right after about a mile. (sign: Milborne St. Andrew)

After about 4 miles, turn right. (sign: Puddletown) A short steep climb levels out into the familiar hedgerows, then into open countryside. You'll encounter a fairly steep hill after a couple of miles that rises for about ½ mile.

At the light, turn left. (signs: Polle, Tolpuddle, Bere Regis) After the initial short climb, the road is fairly level.

After about a mile, take the left toward Wareham at the fork.

After ½ mile, take a left in front of the pretty church of St. John the Evangelist. (sign: Wareham) You'll pass a small cluster of houses and a series of small hills through trees and grasslands. Stately homes dot the hill to your left.

After 2½ miles turn right. (sign: Warmwell) You'll cross two bridges in this fertile country. Canopies of trees shade you briefly, as the road rises a little and crosses the railroad tracks.

At the big roundabout, take the far right path (not the dual carriageway) toward Dorchester (A352). After 1½ miles of closely spaced trees and fields on this sometimes busy road, you come into **Broadmayne**.

This bright little village has many ivy-covered stone houses and a pub called The Black Dog.

In the middle of Broadmayne, turn left at the sign to Preston (also called Chalbry Road). A slight uphill leads you out of the residential area and winds up and down through what was new-mown grass when we last passed. The incline becomes fairly steadily uphill for about ½ mile, cresting to a great view of the Weymouth Bay off to your left. Stay on the main road at this point. You have another moderately climbing hill to cycle with a spreading and spectacular view of the bay. This road straddles a ridge, allowing you to view farms on one side and the sea on the other.

After 5 miles on this road, take a left on the busy A354. (sign: Weymouth)

Take the challenging middle road upward. It climbs steeply for ½ mile. You'll be treated here to a great view of the Dorset countryside before gliding down a long hill. After about 5 miles on this road you come into **Martinstown**.

Take a left here. (signs: Hardy's Monument, Steepleton) A stream follows the road for a short time, as you pedal along past quaint B&Bs. Stay on the main road, which bends and rises gently and takes you, after a couple of miles, into **Winterbourne Steepletown**.

In the middle of town, take a left. (signs: Portesham, Hardy's Monument, Abbotsbury) You'll climb gently but steadily, then up a short steep hill, then more gently again, with a short downhill respite, until the hill crests and the sea becomes visible as you fly downhill into **Portesham**.

Turn left at the sign for Abbotsbury. You'll feel as if you've stepped back into the Middle Ages, only with modern conveniences, as you wend through this village of buff-colored stone houses. The setting couldn't be more exquisite. Right on the sea, with hills rising behind, this village is worth the climbs to reach it.

WHERE TO STAY AND DINE IN ABBOTSBURY

The largest place in Abbotsbury is the Ilcester Arms (tel. [0305]871243) which is right on the main street of the village. This hotel has a good restaurant. They have an assortment of fresh fish every day, and the appetizers are worth a meal in themselves. You might enjoy the smoked mackerel and the grilled avocado Dijonnaise. You can sit in the garden in back and look at the ruins on the hill and the sea in the distance. Beer fans take note: their draught Pilsner is icy cold, a rarity in this land of warm beer drinkers. (Medium)

There are several B&Bs in town. One we liked was the Farmhouse B&B (no telephone), where they take pride in the cream teas they serve.

DAILY SUMMARY

SOUTH OF ENGLAND TOUR

Day Four: Blandford Forum to Abbotsbury

(45–47 miles; moderate)

- Leave on the A354 (sign: Dorchester).
- Go right at the next intersection. After a bit you see and take the little road toward Winterborne Strickland.
- After 5 miles you'll come into Winterborne Strickland.
- Go left here (sign: Milton Abbas).
- Follow the signs through the middle of the village to Milton Abbas.
- After 3 miles, turn right (sign: Milbourne St. Andrew), then immediately right again (sign: Milton Abbas).
- Milton Abbas will appear in 2½ miles.
- Turn left here toward Milton Abbey.
- At the bottom of this residential street, go right (sign: Milton Abbey).
- After touring the abbey grounds, head right to return to Milton Abbas.
- Go right after a mile or so (sign: Milborne St. Andrew).
- After crossing the river, turn left (sign: Milborne St. Andrew).
- After approximately 4 miles, go right (sign: Puddletown).
- At the light after a few miles, turn left (signs: Polle, Tolpuddle, Bere Regis).
- After a mile, head left at the fork (sign: Warcham).
- After ½ mile, turn left in front of the church of St. John the Evangelist (sign: Warcham).
- After 2½ miles, turn right (sign: Warmwell).
- In 5 miles, in Warmwell, take the far right direction at the big roundabout toward Dorchester (A352—don't take the dual carriageway).
- In the middle of Broadmayne, after 1½ miles, go left at the sign to Preston (Chalbry Road).
- After 5 miles, turn left on the A354 (sign: Weymouth).
- In 2 miles, turn right toward Winterbourne Abbas (B3159).
- Take the very steep middle road at this intersection.

- After 5 miles, in Martinstown, go left (signs: Hardy's Monument, Steepleton).
- After 2 miles, in Winterbourne Steepletown, go left (signs: Portesham, Hardy's Monument, Abbotsbury).
- After crossing a hill, in Portesham, go left at the sign for Abbotsbury.
- Turn right shortly (sign: Abbotsbury, Bridport).
- Another 2 miles takes you into Abbotsbury.

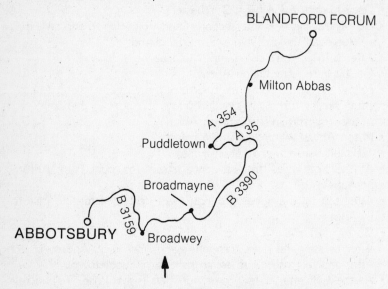

DAY FIVE: ABBOTSBURY TO SHERBORNE (by way of Lyme Regis)

(56 miles; challenging)

This day begins with a seaside jaunt to the town of Lyme Regis. This is your longest day at approximately 56 miles, so we suggest an early start with some snacks packed for extra fuel. Today's ride is challenging in the morning, with a series of steep hills to work off your high teas. The afternoon is moderate with rolling hills. The day starts with a steep climb out of Abbotsbury of about a mile, followed by a long downhill run with the sea to your left and the quilted fields of

Dorset to your right. The fields have low stone walls (rather than high hedges) demarcating their boundaries—which opens the view a great deal.

Your route all the way into Bridport is the B3157. After 4½ miles you'll pass through the village of **Swyre,** followed by another steep climb of about a mile. As you roll over the top, you see the coastline stretches out for miles. The road ribbons downhill, with a sandy beach for a possible morning stroll. Another 3 miles takes you through the outskirts of the little village of **Burton Bradstock.**

Your remaining 3 miles into Bridport pass more glorious seaside and hill country.

As you enter Bridport, take the A35 to your right. (sign: Dorchester) Brick walls enclose the modern houses on your right.

Turn left after about ¼ mile to follow the Town Centre signs. Bridport is a modern seacoast town with shops to stock up on any supplies you need.

At the roundabout go right on the A35. (signs: Exeter, Lyme Regis) There is a moderate uphill for about ½ mile after this turn, followed by a long downhill, with the next village visible in the distance. High hedgerows line this well-paved road where you'll need to watch for occasional heavy traffic (there's no other coastal way to Lyme Regis). About 2 miles from Bridport you come into **Chideock,** another charming coastal village with a preponderance of thatched roofs. You exit the village on a steep uphill for nearly a mile, cresting into **Morcombelake.** You'll smell the ocean and see it on your left, then pass under a roof of trees to enter a sweeping view of checkerboard hills all the way to the horizon on the right. You can rest your legs on this long downhill for over 2 miles. At the bottom of the hill you enter **Charmouth** and begin to climb another steep hill through the good-sized town.

Just out of town take the left fork to Lyme Regis (A3052).
Yet another climb greets you, this one into thick, beautiful
woodlands. You'll glimpse the hills of **Lyme Regis** and come
into the village outskirts after about 1½ miles, on a downhill.
The information center is right on the main street, which becomes steeply uphill in the middle of town.

You may find, as we did, that Lyme Regis is a bit
crowded. However, it is a very pretty town to have a snack
and a stroll, especially if you get off the main street and wan-
der among its twisting lanes and manicured gardens.

At the far side of town, take a right at the sign to Uplyme.
(sign: Hospital) This narrow downhill road takes you two
blocks through a residential area.

Follow the sign left to Uplyme. After less than 1½ miles you
enter **Uplyme** and officially enter Devon. Your route leads
up and down moderate hills and quickly into countryside. The
winding road passes many stone houses with large gardens.
About a mile out of town you enter a wooded area with the
rich smells of earth and long-standing trees. The road is steadily uphill through this section.

**At the intersection, go straight across the busy A35 toward
Crewkerne.** You're riding the crest of a hill here through
houses and hedges within the valley **Marshwood**. You continue downhill through homes and countryside, then up a
short hill into **Birdsmorrgate**.

Turn right at the intersection on B3164. (sign: Broadwindsor)
Stay on the road to Broadwindsor through the high hedges,
as the road bends gently but steadily uphill. After a couple
of miles the hill turns and you roll down and along the gentle
hills of this ridge that opens great scenes with each bend in
the road. About 5 miles from Marshwood is the town of
Broadwindsor.

At the first intersection, turn right. (sign: All other routes,
Beaminster)

After a block turn right toward Beaminster.

Turn left after just a block toward Beaminster. A short downhill and steep uphill take you out of town into a long gliding downhill into **Beaminster.** We suggest stopping for lunch here at the tea shop or inn. There is a great bakery and fruit market, as well as a picturesque restaurant called the Bridgehouse.

Just past the Bridgehouse, take a left toward Evershot on the B3163. You'll leave this officially quaint town by the well-paved road on a steady, gentle uphill through the familiar rows.

At an intersection about 1½ miles outside town, stay on the road to Maiden Newton. The road heads uphill more steeply for ½ mile, then more gently a little farther. A steep downhill and moderate uphill take you over the next beautiful section of Devon hills. After going 3 miles from Beaminster, you come to the next juncture.

Take the road straight across toward Evershot. Your route passes more stone country homes on a slight downhill grade and the occasional stone bridge. Follow the signs to Evershot. The last mile into the village continues to follow up- and downhill with more open pastureland on either side. The next village reached is **Holywell.**

Just out of town, take a right, then an immediate left toward Batcombe. The road is somewhat narrower and continues to follow hill and dale, with a wilder, less cultivated look to the roadside and the fields where sheep and cattle graze. Riding this ridge may challenge your legs but will reward your senses, especially your eyes, with miles-long valley vistas. Stay on the main road, which snakes into shaded woodland then out into more valley views a couple of times before falling steeply downhill.

Take the left turn toward Sherborne at this fork about 4 miles from Holywell (A352). Stay on the A352 for 8 miles into Sherbourne. You'll pass through **Middlemarsh,** with several fine examples of thatched roofs. The road is fairly straightforward and basically level as you stay on the A352 to **Sherborne.** Deep in the heart of Dorset, this city has something for everyone: It houses two castles and an abbey, plus the many beautiful homes you can see while wandering through the back streets. The castles both formerly belonged to Sir Walter Raleigh. The older one was mostly wiped out in the Civil War, but the ruins can still be visited daily from 10 A.M. to 6 P.M. The newer castle was built by Sir Walter later when he saw that his old castle could not be remodeled to please him. Also, Sherborne Abbey is worth a visit.

WHERE TO STAY AND DINE IN SHERBORNE

There is a good place to stay right near the abbey. The Eastbury Hotel (Sherborne, Dorset DT9 3BY; tel. [0935]813131) was built in 1740. Bibliophiles will enjoy the Eastbury's library of rare books. Prices vary greatly depending on your choice of room. (Medium–Top)

DAILY SUMMARY

SOUTH OF ENGLAND TOUR

Day Five: Abbotsbury to Sherborne

(56 miles; challenging)

- You begin and stay on B3157 all the way into Bridport, 10 miles.
- You'll pass Swyre in 4½ miles and Burton Bradstock in another 3.
- In Bridport, take the A35 right (sign: Dorchester).
- After ¼ mile, go left to follow the Town Centre signs.
- Follow the A35 (signs: Exeter, Lyme Regis) at the next two intersections.
- Chideock is 2 miles from Bridport, followed by Morcombelake.

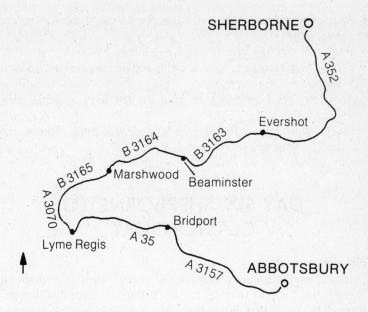

- Just outside Charmouth, turn on the left fork toward Lyme Regis (A3052), which you'll enter in about 1½ miles.
- At the far side of town, take a right at the sign to Uplyme and Hospital.
- Follow the left road to Uplyme, which appears in less than 1½ miles.
- At the next intersection, go across the busy A35 on the B3156 (sign: Crewkerne).
- In 3 or 4 miles you pass through Marshwood, then Birdsmorrgate.
- Take the right on B3164 (sign: Broadwindsor), which is 5 miles from Marshwood.
- At this first intersection, turn right (sign: All Other Routes, Beaminster).
- Turn right toward Beaminster after a block, then left after another block toward Beaminster, which you pedal through in 2 miles.
- Follow the signs to Town Centre.
- Just past the Bridgehouse, turn left on the B3163 (sign: Evershot).
- After 1½ miles, stay on the road toward Maiden Newton.

- After another 1½ miles, take the road straight across toward Evershot.
- You'll ride through Evershot in 3 miles, then Holywell.
- Just outside Holywell, take a right and immediate left toward Batcombe.
- About 4 miles from Holywell, take the left turn on A352 (sign: Sherborne).
- Stay on the A352 for 8 miles into Sherborne, passing Middlemarsh and Longburton.

DAY SIX: SHERBORNE TO GLASTONBURY

(30 miles; moderate)
Today's shorter, easier ride of 30 miles takes you through village and field to that center of Arthurian legend, Glastonbury. The town of Glastonbury has a mystic feel all its own; it's full of legends, including one that claims that Jesus visited this area.

Leave town on the B3148. (sign: Marston Magna) Your first 3 miles roll through the hills and fields you've come to expect.

Turn right at the semiobscured sign for Sanford Orcas. This is a little country lane through the back country, narrowing to one lane at times. Stay on the road to Sanford Orcas, which plunges downhill into **Sanford Orcas.**

At the T intersection, turn left toward Rimpton. The Sanford Orcas Manor House and the magnificent church appear directly on your right, where you may want to stop and explore. Continue on this small road past farms with pastures and flowering vines. Stay on the main road, which takes a left just out of the village (no sign). You may note with relief that the road is basically flat.

A couple of miles outside Sanford Orcas, follow the sign to Rimpton. The road rises briefly over an old stone-walled bridge, then comes into the stone buildings of the outskirts of **Rimpton.**

At the intersection with many choices, go right toward Castle Cary on the A359.

Take the A359 (A303) for less than a mile.

Turn left toward Burton and Frome, then an immediate right to stay on the A359. The road remains essentially flat, with occasional slight rises and one moderate hill about 2 miles past your turn.

Turn left toward Castle Cary on the B3152. After about a mile you come into **Castle Cary.** A large church stands above the town. The George Hotel, right in the center of town, has a large menu of sturdy lunches, including homemade soups and puddings. A few stores up the street a bakery and sweet shop can replenish your glucose needs. Across the street, the Old Bakehouse is a combination natural foods store and café.

After lunch, go back through town to the duck pond, where you'll turn right at the fork. (signs: Shepton Mallet, Bath, Bristol).

Turn immediately toward Bath, Bristol (A371).

Stay on the road to Castle Cary North. These three quick junctions take you out of town.

Turn left after about ½ mile. (railroad station sign).

Turn left again at the T intersection on the B3153. (sign: Somerset) This open flat countryside follows the railroad track for a time, with occasional tall trees in the first mile. The small village of **Alford** has a couple of blocks of stone houses. Then you're back into pastureland and meadow. After another ½ mile you pass through the thatched roofs of **Lovington.** After 2 miles you enter the next village.

In **Lyford on Fosse**, at the light, take the road straight across toward Somerton and Keinville. The houses in the village of **Keinton Mandeville** are especially overgrown with ivy and moss. Stay on the B3153 here. The main road continues on its level way and turns to the left; follow the main road.

Turn right toward Street and Glastonbury. More small hills take you into manicured English fields and the homes of **Street.**

Go straight through the stop light here.

At the roundabout, go right on A39. (sign: Bridgewater)

At another roundabout after a few hundred feet take the sign to Glastonbury, A39.

At the next roundabout, after ¼ mile, take the A361 to Glastonbury. You'll see the town in the distance.

Follow the signs toward Glastonbury Abbey.

WHERE TO STAY AND DINE IN GLASTONBURY

Part of Glastonbury's charm is its combination of ancient and New Age flavor. It's full of crystal shops, natural foods restaurants, and friendly folks with magical and mystical interests. There are probably over a hundred B&Bs in the environs of Glastonbury; we will list a few of the better ones close to the downtown area, and the helpful tourist information center can steer you to others.

In a secluded Victorian house just a few minutes from the central area, Mrs. Butler has a pleasant B&B with a big garden out back, the St. Edmunds House (26 Wells Road; tel. [4058]33862).

A larger house in the Georgian style, the Chalice Hill House on Dod Lane (tel. [0458]32459) has a swimming pool and a large selection of videos for guest use. There is a sauna there, too, if you want to sweat away a few aches.

On the Tor, a popular hiking spot near town, Mrs. Livingstone operates Shambala (tel. [0458]31797), a pleasant cottage with a fine view of the area. Guests here are also welcome to use the kitchen.

The George and Pilgrims Hotel (Glastonbury BA6 9DP; tel. [0458]31146) has been putting up guests since before Columbus set sail for America. In spite of its ancient look, the rooms are equipped with direct-dial phones and private baths. The dining room is good here, too.

The Ploughshares Café serves a substantial array of natural foods dishes, as does their neighbor just up the High Street, Rainbow's End Café. Pizzas on whole-wheat crust, baked potatoes with various stuffings, and other light fare at reasonable prices are the mainstay at these two friendly places.

Fancier dinners are available at several of the local hotel dining rooms, including the establishment called simply No. 3 (it's at 3 Magdalene St.). Here you can get a lobster dinner, fresh fish, or traditional English roast beef. There is a bakery on the High Street, with the interesting name of Burns the Bread. They have an extensive array of Cornish pastries, meat pies, and such, along with sweet baked treats. They have a devoted clientele, too; we had to stand in line to get our goodies last time we were there. (Medium)

WHAT TO DO IN GLASTONBURY

The main attraction here is Glastonbury Abbey, the great goal of pilgrims throughout the Middle Ages. Though only a ruin today, it's a particularly beautiful ruin, with acres of well-tended greens among its monuments. One of the legends that you will hear at the Abbey is that Joseph of Arimethea brought the Holy Grail here (when it was the Isle of Avalon) and buried it at the nearby Tor. Also, Arthur and Guinevere were supposedly buried at the Abbey, where two skeletons were dug up by monks in the twelfth century and relocated to a marble tomb. Once a vastly wealthy and powerful monastery, the Abbey finally fell when Henry VIII closed it down with the rest of the monasteries in England. The last abbot was hanged at the Tor.

Glastonbury has such a mystical atmosphere that it is the kind of place legends ought to happen in. You could spend many hours walking and resting on the expansive grounds of the Abbey. Most visitors feel compelled to climb the Tor, which is about 500 feet high, to visit the thirteenth-century tower at the top and survey the countryside. If you are a museum person, a visit to the Abbey Farm will give you a picture of rural Somerset life over the past century. In the high season there are daily displays of rural crafts such as butter-making and weaving. The museum is only open in the afternoons on the weekend, but from 10 A.M. to 5 P.M. during the week.

DAILY SUMMARY

SOUTH OF ENGLAND TOUR

Day Six: Sherborne to Glastonbury

(30 miles; moderate)

- Exit on B3148 (sign: Marston Magna).
- After 3 miles, go right at the half-hidden sign for Sanford Orcas.
- In Sanford Orcas, turn left toward Rimpton at the T intersection.
- 2 miles outside Sanford Orcas, follow the sign to Rimpton.
- In Rimpton, at the multiple choice intersection, go right on A359 (sign: Castle Cary).
- In 1 mile or so, you'll ride through Queen Camel, then Sparkford.
- Take the A359 (A303) for less than a mile.
- Head left to stay on the A359 (signs: Burton, Frome).

- After a few miles, turn left on the B3152 (sign: Castle Cary), which appears about a mile farther.
- After lunch, go back through town to the duck pond and turn right at the fork (signs: Shepton Mallet, Bath, Bristol).
- Take an immediate left on A371 (signs: Bath, Bristol).
- Stay on the road toward Castle Cary North.
- After ½ mile, go left at the railroad station sign.
- Turn left again at the T intersection on the B3153 (sign: Somerset).
- You'll pass through Alford and Lovington.
- Two miles from Lovington, in Lyford on Fosse, go straight across at the light toward Somerton and Keinville.
- 2½ miles from Keinton Mandeville, turn right toward Glastonbury.
- Follow the signs toward Street and Glastonbury for the few remaining miles.
- At the roundabout, go right on A39 (sign: Bridgewater).
- At the next roundabout, stay on A39 (sign: Glastonbury).
- After ¼ mile, take the A361 at the next roundabout (sign: Glastonbury).
- Follow the signs toward Glastonbury Abbey.

SHAKESPEARE COUNTRY: TOURING THE COTSWOLDS

POINT YOUR BIKE IN ANY DIRECTION HERE, AND YOU WILL find something wonderful. When people go looking for the soul of England, the Cotswolds countryside is one place they always explore. The name itself is evocative. A wold is a high plateau or open land; *cots* is an Old English spelling of "God's." So the Cotswolds are "God's plateaus." It is superb bike-riding territory: Picturesque villages are everywhere and the distances are not great between them. There is a proliferation of tiny back roads, making it easy to avoid the tour buses. This area definitely draws the tourists, especially on weekends and in July and August, so plan your journey accordingly. By sticking to roads such as the ones we lay out in the tour that follows, you will likely encounter crowds only when you stop in the more famous villages.

In addition to the rural feel of this area, its beauty is enhanced by splendid architecture. During the height of the British domination of the wool trade, the Cotswolds' many sheep produced huge surpluses of wool. The sheep barons built many fine houses and endowed their villages with gorgeous churches, some of which are so grand that they almost seem out of place in the modest-sized villages they anchor. Good for you, though, because there is no finer place to stop for a rest than in the gardens of a Cotswold church.

Our tour begins in Cirencester, an ancient hub of Roman activity, and a hub of the increasingly properous area in more recent times. Cirencester used to rank second in size to London. Today this market town is a cosmopolitan center of manageable size where you can find local delicacies alongside international goods of all kinds. We located a splendid coffee, tea, and pastry shop just off the town square, where you can also find the well-stocked tourist information center and a very fine hotel. To reach Cirencester, take the train (Bath–Swindon line), change trains at Swindon and go to Kemble. Take the A429 the 2 miles into Cirencester.

This is a good town in which to acquaint yourself with the distinctive flavor of the Cotswolds and their roots. The excellent Corinium Museum is a good historical source of information about Roman influence and subsequent developments. Many of the side streets look much the same as they did several centuries ago. The church here, a striking example of wool fortune largesse, is the largest in Gloucestershire, dating from the Norman era. You can also stretch your legs in magnificent style in Cirencester Park, a 3,000-acre expanse of lawn, garden, and trees west of town.

We enjoyed a delightful stay in the four-poster suite at the Fleece Hotel, a former coach inn with a lovely indoor courtyard (Market Place, Cirencester, Gloucestershire GL7 2NZ; tel [0285]68507). The staff was especially friendly and helpful, the room was softly and elegantly decorated in blue tones, the bed large and firm. The tariff here includes color TV, direct-dial phones, and sometimes, a phone in the sumptuous bathroom. (Medium–Top)

Another choice is the King's Head (tel. [0285]3322), most of whose seventy rooms come with baths. The menu of this old coach inn is one of its main attractions. (Medium)

DAY ONE: CIRENCESTER TO STROUD

(30 miles; moderate)
Today's 30-mile start is over easy to moderately hilly terrain, with a couple of short challenging climbs. You'll get a good introduction to the splendors of the Cotswolds, with small villages and large cities punctuating the rolling hills.

Leave downtown on the A417 toward Cheltenham. This city road leads through the outskirts of Cirencester. There is a wide sidewalk to the left.

Take a right on the A435 after several blocks. (signs: Baunton, No. Cherney) After ½ mile or so, more trees line the road and you ride into the countryside. The homes have large yards and gardens. You pass the golf course on the left, then the road rises slightly.

After less than ½ mile, turn left on the little road with the sign to Bagendon.

After about a block, turn left at the sign to Daglingworth. You climb a steep hill here with thick forests on the left and open fields on the right. Follow the sign to Daglingworth at the top of the hill, a little less than a mile. Stone walls line the road.

At the intersection with A417, head straight across, following the sign to Daglingworth. The country lane heads ½ mile downhill through hedges into **Daglingworth,** the last village in the Duntisbourne valley, after less than ½ mile. Daglingworth's small Church of the Holy Rood has three excellent examples of simple, moving Saxon sculpture that you may want to see.

Just as you come into town, at the X intersection, turn right at the signs for Sapperton and Stroud.

Take the next road, marked Sapperton, Stroud. Heading uphill again through the stone houses of a little unmarked village, you come into open country quickly. A large house marks the entrance to forest after about a mile on this road. You encounter some slight hills and head into open fields in ¼ mile.

After 1½ miles from the last intersection, take another left toward Sapperton and Stroud at a stone farmhouse. Large trees overhang the road at intervals as you ride through hayfields and hedges. The land is fairly flat, and the road gently snakes through this pastoral scenery.

Stay on the main road until you hit the main Cirencester–Edgewood road, which you'll ride straight across. The road heads downhill toward the woods visible in ¼ mile, then into this deep woodland on a slight uphill and out to the next junction.

At the intersection with A419, go straight across. Golden and green pastures dotted with trees and lined by low stone walls spread out in each direction. A moderate downhill rolls around curves and past the poppies that line the road.

At the X intersection about a mile past the last, go straight across. (sign: Cherington). Mild hills take you through this next section of farmland and the occasional farmhouse, then the road becomes level again after a mile or so. Another two miles take you into **Cherington,** where you turn right at the T intersection toward Avening.

Follow the sign to Avening. For the next 2 miles keep following the signs to Avening. You've come into beautiful forestland here on a narrow road that winds down and up a couple of steep grades and past orchards on your left. A cluster of homes fronts the high stone walls on the left that protect the lovely lowlands. After your next turn wonderful large stone buildings come into view.

Go on into **Avening** if would like to pause for a cup of tea or simply a look around a representative Cotswold village.

Take the B4014 toward Nailsworth. This downhill road leads you past the stone village homes and out into more countryside. You're following the side of a hill with a lovely valley below, then into deep forestland again after a little less than a mile. The level road begins to head on a gentle downslope around winding turns into **Nailsworth,** 2-miles from Avening. Nailsworth has a long, proud industrial past in the wool trade, and is still busy, as many of its cottages have been converted and modernized.

Turn left toward Bath on the A46. This uphill 2-block stretch takes you to a right fork.

Take the B4135 toward Horsley. A short steep hill takes you through the outskirts of Nailsworth and quickly into **Horsley.** A steep uphill leads into the village center, with its stone church and its pub. If you look over the fence you'll see clusters of charming stone houses on the neighboring hills. An uphill takes you out of town.

Take the right fork toward Nympsfield. This tiny road bounces along past low stone walls and fields of growing wheat. The road is a little more hilly here and the territory is wonderfully wild and essentially untrafficked. After 2 miles a steep downhill and up moves into the small stone houses of **Nympsfield.** This is a very pretty little treat to discover in the backroads of England. We recommend stopping for lunch at the large and pleasant Rose and Crown, with its flower planters in front.

At the X intersection, go straight across toward Selsey and Stroud. Vines have overgrown the stone walls in places, and trees lovingly planted years ago line the road.

Take the right on B4066 toward Stroud after less than a mile. You'll come into more forest area with a striking view of the valley to your right as you climb a slight incline for about ¼ mile. You're on the high road here, but as you look off to the left you'll see the huge valley that leads to the Severn

River. The road crests and heads steeply downhill for a couple of miles into **Stroud.**

Keep following the signs into Stroud; going through several roundabouts to the town center. Stroud, nestling in the center of the beautiful Slad Valley, is a large town with lots of history, having been at one time the very heart of the textile industry. There are museums and historic halls, including the Medieval Hall, the oldest building in Stroud, which displays stonework in its carefully restored rooms. There are also many short day trips from Stroud, including Berkeley Castle and several spectacular commons.

WHERE TO STAY AND DINE IN STROUD

Close to the center of town, the Fern Rock House (72 Middle Street, Stroud GL5 1EA; tel [0453]757307) has simple, clean lodging in a Georgian-style house. The Fern Rock can accommodate special diets if you notify them in advance. (low Medium)

About a mile from the town center, the Downfield Hotel (134 Cainscross Road, Stroud GL5 4HN; tel [0453]764496) has about twenty rooms, half of which have bathrooms *en suite*. (Medium)

Also close to the town center, The Old Vicarage (167 Slad Road, Stroud GL5 1RD; tel. [0453]752315) is a secluded former Victorian vicarage with a large garden and TV, telephone, and tea facilities in its three *en suite* rooms. (Modest–low Medium)

Stroud is a big town with many dining options available, including Chinese and Indian cuisine. Gourmet regional cuisine can be sampled at the Oakes (tel. [0453]759950).

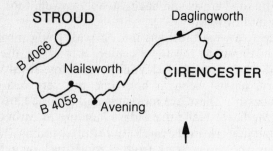

DAILY SUMMARY

SHAKESPEARE COUNTRY TOUR

Day One: Cirencester to Stroud

(30 miles; moderate)

- Leave the downtown area on the A417 toward Cheltenham.
- After several blocks turn right on the A435 (signs: Baunton, No. Cherney).
- After less than 1 mile, go left on the little road (sign: Bagendon).
- After a block, turn left (sign: Daglingworth).
- At the intersection with A417 after about a mile, go straight across (sign: Daglingworth).
- Daglingworth appears in about ½ mile, where you turn right at the X intersection (signs: Sapperton, Stroud).
- Take the next road marked Sapperton, Stroud.
- After 1½ miles, turn left at a stone farmhouse (signs: Sapperton, Stroud).
- Stay on the main road until you reach the main Cirencester–Edgewood Road. Cross this (the sign was broken off the last time we were there, but the road heads downhill).
- Go straight across the intersection with A419.
- After about a mile, go straight across (sign: Cherington).
- 2 miles takes you into Cherington, where you turn right at the T intersection (sign: Avening).
- For the next 2 miles, follow the signs toward Avening.
- In Avening, take the B4014 (sign: Nailsworth).
- In Nailsworth, 2 miles later, go left on the A46 (sign: Bath).

- After 2 blocks, take the B4135 toward Horsley.
- In Horsley, near Nailsworth, take the right fork toward Nymps-
  field, which appears in 2 miles.
- At the X intersection, go straight across (sign; Selsey, Stroud).
- After less than 1 mile, turn right on B4066 (sign: Stroud).
- This road leads downhill into Stroud.

DAY TWO: STROUD TO MALMESBURY

(33 miles; moderate, with challenging sections)
This 33-mile day has a touch of all Cotswold elements—
streams, fields of sheep, rolling hills, pristine stone cottages
and old manor houses—although today's route skirts the
edges of what is properly considered the Cotswolds. Malmesbury and environs are considered Wiltshire country, but in this
tour we want to cover as much of the heartland of England
as time and legs allow. Be advised to eat a hearty breakfast;
calling the first climb challenging is a bit of an under-
statement.

Take the A46 toward Bath at two roundabouts.

**Turn right at the sign to North Woodchester about 2 miles out
of town (signs also say Selsey).** Go all the way to the top of
the hill, a very steep climb. Stroud is down in the valley, and
our route describes a reversal of Newton's discovery: what
went down yesterday must come up today.

Take a right at Selsey Herb Farm. A downhill of less than ½
mile takes you to the corner with a post box on the right.

Turn left on the little road there. There's a great view just
over the stone wall of the valley and Stroud.

Turn left at the sign to Kings Stanley. The road leads downhill
into **Kings Stanley.** You'll pedal past wonderful old stone
houses.

Turn left toward Frocester and Leonard Stanley. Less than ½
mile takes you into **Leonard Stanley.**

Continue to follow the next several signs to Frocester. There
is a residential area for over a mile, then the houses space
out into countryside and hedgerows on a flat, somewhat
bumpy road. You'll be moving at the perfect pace to admire
the unique features of the houses.

Turn right toward Eastington. The Frocester Manor is on your
right. This valley road is level and winds quickly into **Eastington,** about 3 miles from your turn into the valley.

At the roundabout, take the direction toward Frampton. You'll
cross the motorway.

Take the right turn on the A38 toward Glouster for about 100
yards, then take the 4071 left toward Frampton. A little over
a mile takes you into **Frampton-on-Severn.** The main picturesque part of Frampton is off to your left toward the village
green. You'll see swans on the pond and the wildfowl preserve
on the left. Take a loop around this village green, perhaps
walk by the water and feed the ducks, then come back out of
town retracing your route on the 4071.

Turn right on the A38 toward Bristol.

Take the A4135 toward Lower Cam and Ainsley. We have a
short, straightforward run on this larger road before we turn
off into back country again. After 2 miles you come into **Cambridge** (not the home of the university).

Turn left toward Dursley on the A4135 after less than a mile.
You cross over the motorway again and into the countryside
with widening roads and fields. You'll pass through the mod-

ern village of **Lower Cam,** a functional residential area of limited charm. Head out of town on an uphill, forested slope.

Within a mile, turn right on B4060 toward Wotton-under-Edge.

Take a right and a quick left to stay on B4060 toward North Nibley and Wotton-under-Edge. Less than a mile takes you into really beautiful countryside, up a little hill and out into views of the valley and wooded hills. Houses begin to have thatched roofs, high stone walls appear, and the rolling hills with thick borders of lush green trees that ride over the crest of the hill to the old stone rampart will please you. You ride downhill for a stretch, then up a moderate hill bordered by rounded hedges and tall trees. The ancient buildings of **North Nibley** come into view about 3 miles from your turn onto B4060. Each turn of the road brings better views of white and buff stone houses or long views over the valley. You're riding a ridge here that follows the moderately steep hills. Another 1½ miles brings you into **Wotton-under-Edge,** a good-sized town with a combination of ancient architecture and modern conveniences. A set of buildings on Church Street is particularly pleasing, with the feel and look of Oxford colleges.

Follow the sign to Town Centre.

Turn left to stay on B4060. (sign: Kingswood)

Turn left just down the hill at the sign to Yates and Kingswood (B4060). In less than a mile you come through the small village of **Kingswood,** where you keep following the signs to Wickwar and Chipping Sodbury. You'll roll up and down small hills into glorious, more open countryside. You'll pass under a couple of arched stone bridges into the town of **Wickwar,** 3½ miles from Kingswood. The road is fairly flat here for a few miles, passing farmhouses and the hedge borders that surround the rich fields. You'll see several ancient buildings set back from the road. Low hills break up the level nature of the ride at a couple of points, but your ride should be easy for the 8½ miles into **Chipping Sodbury.**

Turn left toward Old Sodbury. We suggest a lunch stop here. There are several hotel restaurants from which to choose. The Portcullis Hotel has a friendly pub and an assortment of pub food. If you're in the mood for something fancy Le Rendezvous is available. We had a very fine meal at the Sultan, an Indian restaurant in a three-hundred-year-old building right on the main street. Light fare can be purchased at the fruit and vegetable shop up the street.

Continue to follow the main road through town for a couple of blocks.

At the roundabout take the direction toward Bath (A46). You're still in the suburbs here, with fields and open land on your right. After 2 miles you come into **Old Sodbury.** Continue into this pretty little village on a moderate upslope and down around the sloping curves of the gorgeous countryside for about a mile.

At the stop light, go straight across on the B4040. (sign: Malmesbury) Many ancient buildings dot the more manicured fields here. You'll pass an old stone tower.

Keep following the signs to Malmesbury.

In the well-groomed village of Acton Turville, turn right toward Malmesbury, then left after a block or so. If you want to take a short detour, you can turn left toward **Badminton** and explore this lovely little village before continuing on to Malmesbury. You come into **Wiltshire** after a mile or so, and pass a redbrick tower next to an old building. The countryside is filled with birds and the sweet smells of grass as the road curves up and down long moderate hills about 3 miles into **Luckington**, where you bend through town and continue taking the road toward Malmesbury. After another 2½ miles the road takes a short, sharp upward bend into **Sherston.** This small town has a large church and several residential streets of stone and gray brick houses. This town is followed closely by the tiny village of **Pichney,** then more rolling woodland

and open field. **Easton Grey** appears briefly as you continue on the B4040. About 16 miles from Chipping Sodbury, you'll enter **Malmesbury.**

WHERE TO STAY AND DINE IN MALMESBURY

At the southern border of the Cotswolds, Malmesbury sits on a hill on the famous Avon River. Malmesbury got its original charter from Alfred the Great in the ninth century, and is celebrated as England's oldest borough. Americans visiting here may be interested to note that Abraham Lincoln's mother came from this town.

Most of the accommodations in Malmesbury are fairly expensive. One of the best is the Knoll House Hotel (Swindon Road, Malmesbury, Wiltshire SN16 9LU; tel [0666]823114). The room are loaded with facilities, including color TV and direct-dial phones. You get a morning newspaper with your breakfast as part of the tariff. (Top)

Quite possibly the best place to stay, though, is about 2 miles away from Malmesbury, and is called the Whatley Manor (Easton Grey, Malmesbury, Wiltshire SN16 0RB; tel [0666]8222888). The beautiful rooms here all come with private baths or showers. The hotel has a swimming pool, a tennis court and well-tended formal gardens. It is well worth its high price. (Top)

A good and interesting place for dinner is the dining room of The Old Bell (tel. [0666]822344), which has been in business for over seven hundred years. It's right in the center of town next to the thirteenth-century abbey. Traditional fare presides here. (Medium)

DAILY SUMMARY

SHAKESPEARE COUNTRY TOUR

Day Two: Stroud to Malmesbury

(33 miles; moderate, with challenging sections)

- Take the A46 toward Bath at the first two roundabouts leaving town.
- Turn right about 2 miles out of town (signs: North Woodchester, Selsey).
- After the steep climb, go right at the Selsey Herb Farm.
- Turn left after less than ½ mile on this little road.
- Turn left again to the sign to Kings Stanley.
- In Kings Stanley, go left toward Frocester and Leonard Stanley.
- After less than ½ mile, in Leonard Stanley, take the route to Frocester.
- Turn right toward Eastington after a little over a mile.
- In Eastington, about 3 miles from your turn into the valley, take the direction toward Frampton at the roundabout.
- Turn right on A38 (sign: Glouster) and then left after 100 yards on 4071 (sign: Frampton). Loop through Frampton-on-Severn and back.
- Turn right on A38 (sign: Bristol).
- Take the A4135 shortly (signs: Lower Cam, Ainsley).
- After Cambridge, which appears in 2 miles, go left on the A4135 in another mile.
- Within a mile from Lower Cam, turn right on B4060 (sign: Wotton-under-Edge).
- Stay on the B4060 with a right and quick left (signs: No. Nibley, Wotton-under-Edge).
- North Nibley is about 3 miles from the juncture with B4060.
- In 1½ miles, in Wotton-under-Edge, follow the Town Centre sign.
- Head left to stay on B4060 (sign: Kingswood).
- Go left just down the hill on B4060 (signs: Yates, Kingswood).
- You'll pedal into Kingswood in less than a mile, where you keep following the signs to Wickwar and Chipping Sodbury.
- In 3½ miles, you'll pass through Wickwar.

- In another 8½ miles, turn left toward Old Sodbury in Chipping Sodbury.
- Follow the main road through town for a couple of blocks.
- Take the A46 at the roundabout (sign: Bath).
- In 2 miles you'll enter Old Sodbury.
- Go straight across the stoplight on B4040 (sign: Malmesbury).
- Keep following the signs to Malmesbury and the B4040 through' Acton Turville, Luckington, Sherston, Pichney, and Easton Grey to Malmesbury, which is 16 miles from Chipping Sodbury.

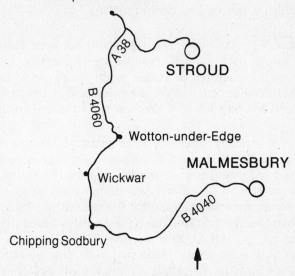

DAY THREE: MALMESBURY TO BOURTON-ON-THE-WATER

(40 miles; moderate)

Today's moderately hilly, 40-mile route takes you into the heart of the Cotswolds, through villages whose perfect beauty postcards can't match. There are many memorable scenes that you will remember long after you return home, culminating in what may be the most glorious village in the whole region, Bourton-on-the-Water.

Leave Malmesbury at the left turn just past town center on the B4040. (sign: Cricklade) A moderate uphill takes you into the countryside.

At the top of this short hill continue on the B4040 toward Cricklade. Shortly out of town you make a right turn following the main road in front of an interesting old building and a long stone wall. Dense areas of forest alternate with long, open fields on this up and down morning.

After about 2 miles, take the right turn to keep following B4040. You'll pass the friendly-looking Horse and Groom pub, where morning tea or coffee might tempt you. Stay on the B4040. You have a couple of moderate hills before leveling out and heading downhill through more pristine farmland.

At the X intersection after 6½ miles or so, go straight across following the B4040 toward Cricklade. Pass over a redbrick bridge and out into the more winding, narrower road moving through the smooth, smaller fields dotted with lazing cattle. Some easy inclines vary the mostly flat road as you cycle past the regular dotting of farmhouses, some with brilliantly colored flowers in front. A mile outside of Cricklade the road rises again at a moderate grade and rolls past a couple of large farms and the Cricklade Country Club before easing downhill into town.

    Cricklade, a fairly large and modern town, has neatly laid-out streets. It is known in part as the first town built on the banks of the here-tiny Thames River, which doesn't become recognizably Thames size until farther down its path.

Take the left just into town to stay on the B4040. This turn takes you through the town center.

Take a right to remain on B4040.

After a couple of long blocks, take the left road fork to follow the sign to Kempsford.

You'll be on the busy A419 for less than ½ **mile (stay on the wide shoulder), then turn right toward Kempsford.** The small road curves and bends through level pastureland and the occasional old stone farmhouse. This is a more rural section of your ride, with grassy green countryside spotted with bushes and tree dividers. Stay on the main road through a couple of side village choices, following the signs to **Kempsford,** where 3 miles on this rural road brings you.

Take the left fork here toward Lechlade.

After two more blocks, take another left toward Lechlade and Fairford. You pass a large airbase on your left leaving Kempsford, and quickly enter **Whelford,** with its beautiful old stone buildings.

Winding and wooded roads take you past dense foliage, landscaped yards, and pubs.

Take a left toward Cirencester. Just ½ mile takes you into **Fairford,** which has a fifteenth-century church, the Church of St. Mary, and many fine old stone buildings. The church has stone angels as timber supports, and the finest stained glass in the region (some say in England). Its vividness and beauty are quite awe-inspiring. We suggest a lunch stop in this lovely town. You can choose from several pubs, including the Bull Hotel. Leo's Restaurant, a fine little establishment, is on the corner of the town square. A well-supplied grocery and fruit and vegetable store can supply your lighter needs. Take some time to walk around this town of many visual treats before heading on.

Take a right at the corner of the town square on the A417 toward Cirencester. The road continues to wind through the ancient stone houses for a couple of blocks.

Take a right here toward Quenington. A slight upgrade takes you through the suburbs and into open land. About 3 miles from Fairford you come into **Quenington**.

Follow the signs here toward Bibury. **Colyn St. Aldwyns** comes along just after Quenington, with many beautiful homes on this upsloping path.

Continue following the signs to Bibury. Just outside of Colyn St. Aldwyns, turn left at the sign to Bibury. This countryside has an older, quainter feel than the section you have been riding through. The woodland glens are tall as the view opens after 2¾ miles into **Bibury.** This is about as perfect and pretty a Cotswold village as anyone is likely to see, shrouded in deep forest, with perfectly clipped hedges, neat stone houses, and a stream running along beside the village. One of its lanes, Arlington Row, belongs to and is preserved by the National Trust.

Turn left at the A433 sign over the bridge and by the Trout Farm.

After exploring this great village, turn back along the stream and head through town.

Turn left at the fork to Aldsworth and Burford (B4425). Leaving town on an upgrade through light forest, you'll crest and enter open country again. The fields are edged with stone walls in places, and the hedges are low enough to allow a clear view of the surrounding countryside. A long downhill and moderate slope covers about a mile, then you'll see another village in the distance. This is **Aldsworth,** about 3 miles from Bibury.

Turn left at the sign to Northleach.

Take a right fork immediately toward Bourton-on-the-Water. This little lane takes you through Aldsworth and uphill a short distance. You'll see evidence of the somewhat drier climate here in the variations on gold and green of the fields. Essentially level, with slight hills, this route rolls through prime sheep grazing land.

After nearly 3 miles, turn left on the A40. (sign: Cheltenham)

After about a mile, turn right toward Sherborne. The trees rise up thickly close to the road here, which bends downhill through pines and flowering hedges.

At the X intersection after a mile, go straight across toward Bourton-on-the-Water. More forested land accompanies the gentle upgrade as you ride past an old stone farmhouse. This is moderately hilly country with very high hedges which act as windbreaks.

Continue following the signs to Bourton-on-the-Water. The valley lands of the Windrush River roll off to your right as you cycle along the crest of the hill.

Keep heading downhill to the right at the fork. A long, shaded downhill takes you the remaining miles of the 4½-mile jaunt into **Bourton-on-the-Water.**

Bourton-on-the-Water, situated on the Windrush River, is an ideal place to spend the night and get a flavor of life in the Cotswolds. Bourton-on-the-Water is an exceptionally pretty village. The great beauty of the Cotswolds is due in part to the natural limestone with which most of the buildings are constructed. The Windrush River, here more a stream, wends its way right through the center of town. The environs of Bourton are ideal for evening strolls along the quiet lanes.

WHERE TO STAY AND DINE IN BOURTON-ON-THE-WATER

Two larger hotels can be recommended.

The Old New Inn (tel. [0451]20467) on the High Street, has twenty-four rooms (eight with private bath) and a good restaurant. Its name reflects the combination of eighteenth-century Queen Anne decor and modern additions. A further attraction of this hotel is a charming model village in the garden. (Medium)

The Dial House Hotel (tel. [0451]22244) has ten rooms and a restaurant that is highly regarded by the locals. (Medium)

There are also many B&Bs in the area. Springfield Close, located just as you come into town (tel. [0451]22373), is comfortable and quiet. Just up the street is a real charmer called Sherborne House (tel. [0451]20170). It has a beautiful garden complete with roaming chickens.

The Windrush Restaurant, which is right in the center of town, has outdoor dining and a variety of light fare. (Modest–Medium)

The Old Bakery (tel. [0451]21168) was especially welcome to us after a long day of Cotswold country air. There is a charming set of rooms up under the eaves here, plus an ironing board and other amenities for boarders. (Medium)

The Rose Tree (tel. [0451]20635), also highly regarded by both locals and visitors, has a dual attraction with its centuries' old cottage in a riverside setting and its fresh and selective menu. Outdoor tables are available here when the weather permits. This is one restaurant where reservations can assure you of a great dining experience. (Medium)

WHAT TO SEE AND DO IN BOURTON-ON-THE-WATER

In addition to the model village, Bourton has a model railway, motor museum, and Birdland and Folly Farm, bird preservation centers, to explore. The four hundred square feet of track and scenery and forty-plus trains comprising the model railway will delight locomotive buffs. The shop has toys and essential train paraphernalia for the entranced fan. Birdland is not only beautiful but useful; it houses and protects a range of endangered wildfowl species from around the world. You can see flamingos and penguins, parrots and herons, all in the same place. The eighteenth-century watermill that houses the motor museum is interesting in itself, and the museum stores motoring lore and artifacts of all kinds, along with vintage cars. Folly Farm, a delightful habitat for endangered domestic waterfowl, is set in a natural environment that is very restful.

DAILY SUMMARY

SHAKESPEARE COUNTRY TOUR

Day Three: Malmesbury to Bourton-on-the-Water

(40 miles; moderate)

- Leave Malmesbury on the B4040, just past the town center (sign: Cricklade).
- Continue on the B4040 toward Cricklade after the first hill and at the next junction in 2 miles.
- At the X intersection after 6½ miles, go straight across to stay on B4040 (sign: Cricklade).
- In Cricklade, about 12 miles from Malmesbury, take a left and right to remain on B4040.
- After 2 long blocks, take the left fork (sign: Kempsford).
- Stay on the shoulder of the A419 for less than ½ mile, then go right toward Kempsford.
- You'll reach Kempsford in 3 miles, where you take the left fork toward Lechlade.
- After 2 more blocks, turn left again (signs: Lechlade, Fairford).
- Whelford appears quickly, where you turn left toward Circencester.
- After ½ mile you'll ride into Fairford.
- Go right at the town square corner on A417 (sign: Circencester).
- After a few blocks, head right toward Quenington, which you reach after 3 miles.
- Follow the signs here toward Bibury.
- In Colyn St. Aldwyns, and also after, keep following the signs to Bibury.
- After 2¾ miles, in Bibury, turn left on A433 by the Trout Farm to explore, then turn around back through town.

- Take the left fork on B4425 (signs: Aldsworth, Burford).
- After 3 miles, in Aldsworth, go left (sign: Northleach).
- Take an immediate right fork toward Bourton-on-the-Water.
- After almost 3 miles, turn left on A40 (sign: Cheltenham).
- Turn right toward Sherborne after a mile.
- At the X intersection in a mile, head straight across toward Bourton-on-the-Water.
- Continue following the signs over the hills toward Bourton-on-the-Water.
- At the fork, head on the right, downhill road 4½ miles into Bourton-on-the-Water.

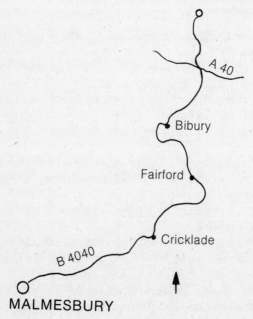

BOURTON-ON-THE-WATER

A 40

Bibury

Fairford

Cricklade

B 4040

MALMESBURY

DAY FOUR: BOURTON-ON-THE-WATER TO CHIPPING NORTON

(42 miles; moderate to challenging)
You could almost think of the past few days as a warm-up
for this one—for your eyes and your legs. Today you will
feast your eyes on a castle and on the village that some people
think is the most beautiful in the Cotswolds. Even the names
of today's villages fall sweetly on the ear: Chipping Camden,
Stow-on-the-Wold, Winchcombe, Upper Swell. In the 42
miles of today's ride you'll alternate level areas with stretches
of rolling hills and some moderately challenging sections.

**Head out of town with the clock tower of St. Lawrence's church
on your right.** Several blocks with more B&Bs follow.

Turn right toward Stow on the A429.

Take the first left toward Naunton. Head toward Naunton on
a slight upgrade through fields that had blooming poppies
when we passed through. (If you want to take a brief detour,
take the right and tour Upper Slaughter, then retrace your
steps and follow the route to Naunton.) You'll pass a small
cluster of limestone houses, and then head back into the richly
green hills of the valley.

After 2 miles, go left at the X intersection. A long downhill
winds through this lush land.

After ½ mile turn right toward Naunton on the little lane.
Another ½ mile takes you into the quaint little village of
Naunton. A short climb takes you through town, where you
won't find many tourists, but will see and hear the essence of
the Cotswolds along the tiny paths between the rowhouses.
Naunton is also home to a famous seventeenth-century dove-
cote which stands, in some disrepair, near the church. Leave
the village on a hill (about a mile long) with stone walls and

the Windrush Valley to your right. Woods crowd the hills beyond.

At the top swing right toward Guiting Power. A downhill of about ½ mile takes you to the T intersection.

Turn right toward Guiting Power. Keep following the signs to Guiting Power.

Turn left at the X intersection after a little more than ½ mile. You come quickly into the ancient homes and church of **Guiting Power.** This village has a special kind of perfection that is enlivened by the modern reality of lives being spent in its proportioned homes and fields. The Cotswold Farm Park occupies an ecological niche here in the heart of the Cotswolds. Home to rare species and historical breeds of farm animals, the Park is open spring through fall (tel. [04515]307). You leave town on a slight uphill with a huge old tree on your left. Gentle hills lead through light forest to an X intersection.

Go straight across and uphill toward Winchcombe. The steep uphill crests after ¾ or 1 mile and moves over the fields past thick forest on either side. The grade continues to be slightly uphill, then up and down dale through flowering hedges with fields beyond. Continue following the signs to Winchcombe. After 3 miles you take a steep downhill with the villages of the valley visible in the far distance. You'll pass a great B&B on the right and may want to stop on this downhill to appreciate the gorgeous valley ahead—the justifiably famous Vale of Evesham. Another 1½ miles brings you through the village of **Winchcombe** to Sudeley Castle.

Follow the signs to visit this large site. This castle is definitely worth a visit. For the somewhat steep sum of £3.75, you can visit a thousand years of British history. The castle has hosted many chapters of historical intrigue. Originally owned by the wonderfully named Ethelred the Unready, it is most famous as the final resting place of Queen Catherine Parr, one of the wives of Henry VIII. In addition, the good-sized castle was the inspiration for P. G. Wodehouse's "Blandings." The large, formal gardens around Sudeley would be a good reason to visit all by themselves. The trees have been carefully tended through many generations, and the grounds are very restful. There is a restaurant and shop on the premises.

Head left out of Sudeley to the village of Winchcombe.

Wind your way up through the village.

Turn right at the T and go through town.

After several long blocks you'll see a sign on your left confirming that you're on the B4632. (sign: Stratford) You can visit a pottery shop just out of the village, then continue on this wider road through low hills, with villages and groves on the slopes. After 2½ miles you come into **Toddington.**

Take the direction at the roundabout toward Broadway. The road dips and rises through slight hills, with views of great slopes and valleys, especially to your right.

Continue following the road toward Stratford and Broadway. The countryside here has a majestic feel to it, with long views and stately trees overlooking the prosperous valley homes. After 4 more miles you come into the famous village of **Broadway.**

Turn right toward the village center. The village is a real treat to the eye: every building seems to match the others perfectly, and the mullioned windows of many buildings are especially attractive. Beware, however, arriving on a weekend or practically any time during July and August. Every tourist bus in the region stops here. Our route uses back roads to get in and out of Broadway. It makes an excellent lunch stop, with many places from which to choose. One particularly nice restaurant is the Hunter's Lodge Restaurant (tel. [0386]853247). If the weather is nice, you can eat in the pleasant garden,

choosing from a menu of fresh produce served with a continental flair.

After exploring this most renowned village in the Cotswolds,
turn on the road to Snowshill. Many thatched-roof cottages
line the uphill road out of the village. The smooth road heads
moderately then steeply uphill for about a mile, with the valley rolling off to the right into **Snowshill.**

Turn right on the fork to Ford and Snowshill. You'll be delighted at the pretty grayish houses and hauntingly handsome
church of this little village, which has a sixteenth-century
manor owned by the National Trust, full of a somewhat dis-
concerting collection of oddments and relics. The gardens are
obviously lovingly tended, with brilliant colors spilling over
the stone walls. You'll have another short, steep climb just
outside the village.

Turn right at the T junction ½ mile out of the village toward
Ford. There's a lovely stretch of fields here through the rolling
hills, where a horse rider waved us on past. Stay on the road
toward Ford on this often quite narrow road. Back through
Toddington briefly, you come out into peaceful pastoral land
along a level lane. There's a special cluster of houses off to
the left through the fields.

Turn right here, 3 miles out of Snowshill, toward Ford.

After a few hundred yards, turn left toward Stow and Ford.
The road bends downhill here, with signs to the Cotswold
Farm Park, where you can stop to visit the rare animals.
Climbing a short hill you come into **Ford.** A wider thoroughfare leads through deep woodland over a few slight hills. You
cycle into more open pastureland following the signs and
stone walls toward Stow-on-the-Wold. You'll begin to see
signs of civilization on the ridge to your right, as hills continue
to unfold peaceably through the farmland. After 6 miles you
pass through **Upper Swell,** a small village, then the road takes
a short hill up by a walled estate on the right. The upgrade

continues for a little over a mile. You then come into **Stow-on-the-Wold,** the highest town in the Cotswolds, where you may want to stop for tea at the Rafters, famous for its timbered charm.

Turn right on the A36 toward Chipping Norton.

After a couple of blocks turn left toward Chipping Norton. The wide road skirts the hill then descends on a gradual then moderate grade past signs to Upper and Lower Oddington. You may want to consider a short detour to explore the primeval feeling of the fourteenth-century wall painting in the church at Oddington. More moderate up- and downhills follow over the wooded land, with a particularly long climb about 3 miles from the village. Continue following the signs to Chipping Norton on this same road for another mile.

Turn right on the A44 toward Osford and Chipping Norton. The wide road with a marked shoulder heads downhill over the first mile, with ancient buildings in the village of Salford to your left. The road continues through even greener fields. A slow uphill has a path off the road that takes you a few hundred yards into the environs of **Chipping Norton.**

Chipping Norton has been a major market town of the area for hundreds of years. "Chipping" is actually derived from the earlier "cheapen," the word for market. Antiquity buffs also seek it out because of the Rolright Stones, often called "The Stonehenge of the Cotswolds." Many interesting buildings brighten the town, including the eccentric and unwieldy Bliss Valley Tweed Mill from the Victorian era. In contrast to the expected limestone manor houses of the area, most of the elegant homes here are Georgian. It is a handsome town, affectionately known to the locals as Chippy, with plenty of opportunities for lodging and dining.

WHERE TO STAY AND DINE IN CHIPPING NORTON

The obvious choice in town for a large hotel is the White Hart, which dominates the central square of the town (High

Street, Chipping Norton, Osfordshire OX7 5AD; (tel. [0608]3572). It has twenty-two bedrooms, six with private baths. If you arrive early enough, you might be able to get one of the two that are furnished with four-poster beds. (Top)

On the opposite end of the price scale is Lemington House (Worcester Road, Chipping Norton OX7 5XX; tel. [0608]641548), which is a bed and breakfast run by a friendly couple. (Modest)

Just outside of town is the Southcombe Guesthouse (tel. [0608]643068). Standing on its own grounds of three acres near a golf course, the Southcombe caters to nonsmokers.

Chipping Norton goes to bed early, so there are not many restaurants open at night. The local Indian restaurant, the Anarkali, serves until late at their location in the center of town. The Blue Boar is also open in the evening.

DAILY SUMMARY

SHAKESPEARE COUNTRY TOUR

Day Four: Bourton-on-the-Water to Chipping Norton

(42 miles; moderate to challenging)

- Leave town with the St. Lawrence's church clock tower on your right.
- Turn right after several blocks on the A429 (sign: Stow).
- Take the first left toward Naunton.
- Go left at the X intersection after 2 miles.
- In another ½ mile, go right on the little lane (sign: Naunton), which you reach in less than ½ mile.
- A mile out of Naunton, go right toward Guiting Power.
- After ½ mile, turn right toward Guiting Power.
- Turn left at the X intersection, after a little more than ½ mile, which takes you into Guitiing Power.
- Go straight across the X intersection toward Winchcombe.
- In 1½ miles you'll come to Winchcombe and Sudeley Castle.

- Leave Sudeley to your left and wind through Winchcombe, turning right at the T intersection.
- After several long blocks a sign confirms your ride on the B4632 (sign: Stratford).
- In 2½ miles, in Toddington, take the roundabout direction toward Broadway.
- Continue following the signs the 4 miles into Broadway.
- Turn right toward the village center.
- Head on the road toward Snowshill, which you'll ride into in a mile.
- Go right on the fork toward Ford and Snowshill.
- After ½ mile, turn right at the T intersection (sign: Ford).
- Riding through Toddington again, turn right 3 miles from Snowshill toward Ford.
- After a few hundred yards, go left (signs: Stow, Ford).
- This road leads through Ford, Upper Swell, and after another mile or so into Stow-on-the-Wold.
- Turn right on A36 (sign: Chipping Norton), and left after 2 blocks.
- After a mile, go right on A44 (signs: Osford, Chipping Norton) the last couple of miles into Chipping Norton.

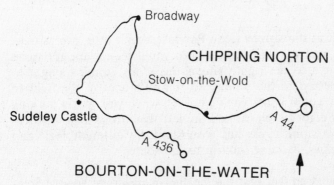

DAYS FIVE AND SIX: CHIPPING NORTON TO STRATFORD

(20 miles; easy to moderate)
Today we leave the Cotswolds proper toward a destination that draws practically everyone who comes to the U.K.

Stratford-upon-Avon is a great place to end the tour, in part
because there is so much to do there and in part because
there are many day trips available in the area, should you
decide to stay an extra day or two. For example, Warwick
Castle is a day loop of about 20 miles. One could easily spend
a whole morning or afternoon exploring this huge attraction
that has been called the finest medieval castle in England.
Today's approximately 20-mile route zigzags through more
beautiful villages with sights to explore on easy to moderate
roads. We begin today by dropping back a few thousand years
with a visit to the Rolright Stones.

Leave town on the Overtown Road.

Turn left on the B4026 toward Overnorton. ½ mile out of
town you climb a short, steep hill into **Overnorton.** This pleasant, tiny village has many stone houses in its curving streets.

Follow the signs to Stratford.

Turn left onto A34.

Turn left at the sign to Little Rollright after a little over a mile.
A little over a mile from the turn you'll see an upright stone
in the field to the right. This is the Kings Stone, thought to
be connected to the unmarked ring of stones in the field to
the left. You'll know you've arrived when you spot a parking
area for eight to ten cars on the left. Due to its isolated location, this stone circle has a substantially different feel than
Stonehenge, its larger cousin to the south.

**A few hundred feet past the monument turn right toward Ship-
ston.** This road heads downhill through tree canopies into **The
Hollows.**

Turn left on the A34 toward Shipston. There is a beautiful
church and many thatch-roofed stone houses. The countryside
is lush and very pleasing to the eye as the wide road with
marked shoulders heads up and down moderate hills. There

are visual treats around each bend, including an unusual turreted house and vine-covered trees. There is a shoulder down the right-hand side of the road for most of the route, if you want to stay off the main road. Large and prosperous churches and farms edge the outskirts of **Shipston-on-Stour,** about 6 miles from The Hollows.

In town, turn left on the B4035. (sign: Campden) The road out of town is slightly uphill through the suburbs and the industrial area, then turns into sweet views of open fields. Snaking along on basically level land, you come to an intersection after almost 2 miles.

Take the road straight across to stay on the B4035. (sign: Chipping Campden) You'll head up a long hill to pass a sign welcoming you to Gloucestershire.

Turn left toward Chipping (4 miles). The narrow road here follows slight hills past Charington Manor, then takes a steep short downhill to view tall cypresses marching up the hill to your right. In season, there is an occasional fruit stand along the road. You'll rise to cross an old stone bridge, then come into a more populated area.

After 4 miles on this road you enter **Chipping Campden.** This town has many well preserved examples of the homes of the Middle Ages, including the ancient Woolstaplers Hall Museum, packed to its roof with bizarre relics and artifacts, such as primitive dental implements. The church here is especially fine, with brass and various monuments to be seen. You may also be interested in visiting Kiftsgate Court Gardens, a superbly situated house valued for its views and three-generation garden with unusual plants and roses. Turn left to go into the main section of town for lunch, which is available at the Bantam Tearoom, Joel's Pizza, or any of several pubs. There is a large bakery around the corner from the Red Lion.

After lunch, turn around to head toward Mickleton on the B4081.

A mile out of town, take the right fork toward Mickleton and Stratford. Your route is still through hilly country, but not too difficult. Vine-covered homes with large overflowing gardens dot your route.

After 2½ miles, take the right fork toward Stratford on the B4632. You're pedaling through the small streets of **Mickleton** for a few blocks.

Turn left to stay on the B4632 toward Stratford.

Take a right turn after ¼ mile to stay on B4632. Keep following the signs to Stratford through this more civilized and level landscape. The hedges are evenly trimmed in sections, and over them you'll see large working farms and open and beautiful hills. You pass a greenhouse on the left which may supply some of the outstanding plants you'll have the pleasure of seeing in gardens along the way. About 6 miles from Mickleton the road comes up a short rise and joins the A34.

Turn left toward Stratford.

Follow the signs to Town Centre.

WHERE TO STAY AND DINE IN STRATFORD

As you come into town there is a solid row of bed and breakfasts for a couple of blocks on both sides of the street. Stratford probably has more accommodations per square foot than any place in England. Here are a few that we can recommend.

Just before you turn onto the A34, you'll see a sign for a B&B with the charming name of Cross o' th' Hill Farm (tel. [0789]283322). It is on a working farm and run by the gracious Mrs. Jones. (Modest–Medium)

The White Swan (Rother Street, Stratford, CV37 6NH; tel. [0789]297022) was over a hundred years old when William Shakespeare was a hot new playwright. Like most places in Stratford, it is rather pricey, particularly for a double. (Top)

Another hotel older than the Bard and carrying his name is the Shakespeare (Chapel St.; tel. [0789]294771). Its sixty-six rooms all have private baths and its bars are particularly genial.

A reasonably priced hotel is the Stratford House (Sheep Street, CV37 6EF; tel. [0789]68288), which is only a few hundred feet from the river and the Royal Shakespeare Theatre. The price includes breakfast. (Medium)

Close in and tiny, the Eastnor Guest House is quite comfortable (Shipston Road, Stratford-upon-Avon, CV37 7 LN; tel. [0789]68115). It is a good bargain. (Medium)

Almost everyone finds their way at some time to the Black Swan (tel. [0789]297312), also known as The Dirty Duck. The food is good here, particularly the appetizers, and on a nice day you might be lucky enough to snag an outdoor table in the garden.

Many of the actors from the theater have their late dinners at Don Giovanni (tel. [0789]297999). As the name implies, this restaurant has an Italian focus. If you are fans, as we are, of that transcendent Italian dessert, zabaglione, it is served here with a flourish. The Theatre itself has a fine restaurant with views overlooking the Avon.

WHAT TO DO IN STRATFORD

The big attraction here is the Bard, of course, who was married and buried here, and in particular the Royal Shakespeare Theatre. Even if you're not a Shakespeare student or fan, we highly recommend an evening in this wonderful theater. The actors are breathtakingly good at what they do. Calling ahead for tickets is a good idea (tel. [0789]295623). The house where Shakespeare lived, and that of his mother, are open to the public and interesting in their detail and surprising smallness (for a man of such large genius).

The River Avon supplies a lot of entertainment all by itself in Stratford. You can picnic along its banks, enjoying the breeze through the overhanging trees. You can tour in large or small boats along its length, imagining the sights and sounds that have crowded its banks over the centuries.

A DAY LOOP TO WARWICK CASTLE

When in Stratford, you are very close to the most famous medieval castle in England. Sir Walter Scott called Warwick Castle "the most noble sight in England." It is huge and deserves the better part of a day to see it. You can stroll its grounds accompanied by peacocks, tour a dungeon, and see the great hall where many royal balls have taken place over the centuries. It also contains a Madame Tussaud exhibit of twenty-nine wax portraits through twelve rooms of the castle.

It's only a 15-mile ride, but it's worth going early in the day so you have ample opportunity to explore the castle.

Take the B4086 to Wellsbourne. This busy road has a good shoulder through town, then comes out into more countryside, with an opportunity to visit Charcote Park (tel. [0789]470277], a highly decorated sixteenth-century house where Elizabeth I was regally entertained and in whose magnificent park Shakespeare is reputed to have poached deer. You can watch a video evoking the Victorian era in this house; a pleasant restaurant in the Orangery serves teas and coffees.

In Wellsbourne, turn left on the A429 to Warwick and take it all the way into Warwick, following the signs to the castle.

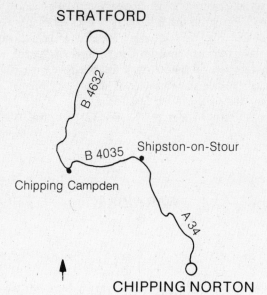

STRATFORD

B 4632

B 4035   Shipston-on-Stour

Chipping Campden

A 34

CHIPPING NORTON

DAILY SUMMARY

SHAKESPEARE COUNTRY TOUR

Day Five: Chipping Norton to Stratford

(20 miles; easy to moderate)

- Leave Chipping Norton on the Overtown Road.
- Go left on B4026 (sign: Overnorton).
- In Overnorton, after ½ mile, follow the signs to Stratford.
- Turn left on A34.
- Go left at the sign to Little Rollright after a little more than a mile.
- A few hundred feet past the Rolright Stones, turn right (sign: Shipston).
- In The Hollows, turn left on A34 (sign: Shipston).
- After 6 miles, in Shipston-on-Stour, go left on B4035 (sign: Campden).
- At the intersection in 2 miles, go straight across on B4035 (sign: Chipping Campden).

- Turn left toward Chipping, which appears in 4 miles.
- Head out of Chipping on the B4081 (sign: Mickleton).
- 1 mile out of town, go right toward Mickleton and Stratford.
- In 2½ miles, take the right fork on B4632 (sign: Stratford).
- In Mickleton, turn left on B4632 (sign: Stratford).
- Turn right after ¼ mile to remain on B4632.
- Keep following the signs toward Stratford.
- About 6 miles from Mickleton, the B4632 joins the A34 into Stratford.

WARWICK

A 429

B 4086

STRATFORD

THE LAKE DISTRICT

LONG FAVORED BY POETS AND HIKERS, THE ENGLISH LAKE District is perfect territory for cycling, too. The challenge for the cyclist here, as in much of the prime territory of the U.K., is to find the back ways that will give you the striking character of the region without encountering too many other tourists. In three separate tours of the Lake District since 1980, we think we have found such a route through this magnificent area.

The Lake District is particularly beautiful in spring and autumn. Spring, with its incredible lushness, and autumn, with its contrast of colors, give a breathtaking character to this region of hill, valley and water. One of our tours here was in May, another in September, and the third in June. Of these three, all of which were fine, the May trip really stands out in our minds as the one with the most grip on our senses.

One thing you will probably notice in this region is the number of hikers. The English are a devoted breed of hikers, and no area draws them more than the Lake District. Now, with the advent of the mountain bike, you will also see quite a few fat-tired fans up here, too. All this outdoor activity gives the region a special flavor, reminding us of Alpine regions of Switzerland and Austria, with the streets full of healthy people wearing backpacks.

This area has its own language of sorts. It took us awhile to figure out the difference between a *mere* and a *tarn* (the former is a lake, the second a small lake). Likewise, a *fell* is a mountain, a little stream is a *beck*, and a waterfall is a *force*.

Wordsworth grew up here (in fact, you can visit the elementary school where he carved his name on a desk), but others such as Thomas De Quincey and Samuel Taylor Coleridge came here and were inspired. Later, Peter Rabbit's creator Beatrix Potter was a devotee of this area as well. The region is not far as the crow flies from the intensely-industrialized regions of Manchester and Birmingham; some poets have even spoken of the difference between the Lake District and the industrial Midlands as heaven and hell. There is some accuracy to this description. On our most recent trip we came across the industrial area to get to the Lake District, and it felt like approaching the gates of heaven when we came over a hill and got our first look at Lake Windermere.

If you are coming to the Lake District by train, come into the station at Oxenholme instead of Kendal. The two stations are only a couple of miles apart, but Oxenholme has direct service, whereas Kendal is on a branch line. If you want to catch the branch train on into Kendal (for example, if the weather is bad), you may be in for a little wait. Trains from London to the Lake District leave Euston Station.

We begin our tour of this magnificent area in Kendal, which is the southern gateway town to the Lake District. Kendal has about twenty thousand full-time residents, many of whom work in the tourist trade in one way or another. Kendal has been an important town for nearly a thousand years. The Normans built a castle here in the twelfth century, and you can still see a cross shaft dating from the ninth century in the local parish church. Later, Kendal became a major center of the wool trade and is even mentioned as such in Part I of *Henry IV*. Nowadays, the town is known as a jumping-off place for tours of the Lake District, and for Kendal Mint Cake, which has accompanied mountaineers on many conquests. Sir Edmund Hilary munched it on his way to the first Everest ascent. It is a slab of rock-hard mint candy, very sweet and quite popular among trekkers.

If you did not bring a mountain bike, this area may make you wish you had one. If so, there are many places to rent them for a day or two, particularly around Windermere. There are scores of bridle paths that crisscross the Lake District, which are ideal for mountain biking. Mountain bikes are not allowed on the byways marked Public Footpaths. These are reserved for hikers, and cyclists should respect this holy tradition which has been a mainstay of this area's draw for two centuries.

GETTING TO KENDAL

From the train station by bicycle, the most direct route is to turn right as you exit the Oxenholme station. The initial road turns and heads downhill into the outskirts of Kendal.

At the T intersection after a mile, turn right on the A65 toward Kendal.

Follow the signs to Abbot Hall and Windermere.

WHERE TO STAY AND DINE IN KENDAL

The helpful tourist information service can book accommodations for you. It is located in the Town Hall on the corner of Highgate and Lowther Street, which is easily identified by the clock tower on top.

Our favorite place to stay in this area is a perfect little country hotel located on a working farm just outside Kendal, called the Lane Head House (Helsington, Kendal, Cumbria LA9 5RJ; tel. [0539]731283), located on the A6 on the opposite side of Kendal from Oxenholme train station. Each spotless room comes with private, sumptuous bath, TV, and direct-dial phones. The scenery from the windows over the formal English garden to the valley beyond is very restful. (Medium)

If you want to stay in the commercial town of Kendal, the Woolpack Hotel is considered the best lodging (Stricklandgate, Kendal, Cumbria LA9 4ND; tel. [0539]23852). Its fifty-seven *en suite* rooms can be expensive, but full English breakfast is included in the rate. The former function of the hotel's bar as a wool auction room gives the hotel its name; the dining room here has a good reputation (Medium–Top)

There are quite a number of B&Bs, one of which is on the way into town from the railroad station. The Riverside Hotel (tel. [0539]724707) also comes highly recommended.

Moon is considered the best restaurant in town (tel. [0539]29254). This restaurant serves innovative cuisine tending toward the vegetarian and natural foods part of the spectrum. (We noticed an entire publication in the tourist information office listing vegetarian establishments in the Lake District.)

DAY ONE: KENDAL TO AMBLESIDE

(34 miles; moderate to challenging)
Your first day's ride in this strikingly beautiful area is approximately 34 miles, with several short stretches of moderate to challenging climbs. In general, Lake District routes will be moderately hilly. (A couple of days have short, steep hills that couldn't be avoided.) Today, you'll enter quickly into the backroads beauties of this area, winding around to spend the night in the bustling little town of Ambleside.

Leave downtown Kendal on Lowther Street, right by the tourist information center, heading toward the sign that says Hospital. You'll climb steeply out of the town for a short distance.

After ¼ mile, follow the signs to the right toward Crosthwaite. The road continues uphill, not as steeply, and crests over into a beautiful little valley ribboned with stone walls. A stone bridge crosses the A591, then you head uphill again on another steep, short climb. After 1 mile of climbing you have a downhill run with the first really good view of the Cumbrian hills crisscrossed with stone fences. Keep following the signs to Crosthwaite. The bramble-lined road is quite winding and consistently downhill for over a mile. You come into **Underbarrow** after another ½ mile, and ride over small hills past lovely old stone farms and thick foliage. The undulating hills take you around the valley in a generally upward direction with several great-looking B&Bs on the way. Finally, 1½ miles past Underbarrow, you come into **Crosthwaite.**

Take the right fork here toward Bowness. The Punchbowl Inn can serve you some morning refreshments. The school here is a combination of ancient stone and modern additions.

Take the left fork at the sign to Bowland Bridge in town. You'll head uphill again over a moderately challenging, but short climb.

At the top of the hill, turn left toward Lyth Valley and Grange. An immediate downhill then moves into gently undulating hills past fields of sheep and groves of trees perched on the top. After a little over a mile you enter a rollercoaster-like section. One challenging uphill brings you another spectacular view of the countryside and the working farms of the area.

At the stop sign turn right toward Barrow on the A590.

Turn right at the sign to Cartmel after about a mile. This one-lane hedgerow takes you uphill rather steeply for less than ½ mile with the rich valley below. A rolling downhill brings you past some lovely homes and fields. You're pedaling downhill or levelly along the snaking road.

Turn left after 1½ miles toward Witherslack. Less than a mile brings you into the small roads past an old farm and gently up over small hills.

At the fork, turn left toward Witherslack. This wonderful back road curves through glorious views of the countryside up and down dale. You come into deep woodlands over small hills with a public footpath, first to your left and later to your right. Leaving the deep forest after a mile, you head downhill into more open fields edged by the forest. The wider pavement here reenters light forest with fields and bluffs visible through trees. A winding uphill takes you past South View Cottage into **Witherslack,** 2 miles from your last fork. This village is spread out along the hilly road. Stay on the main road here, as it comes to a major intersection just past the Derby Arms Hotel.

Take a right on the busy A590 toward Grange and Newby Bridge. We'll take you off this road as soon as possible. Use the wide shoulder.

After a mile, at the roundabout, take the B5277 toward Grange. You're in the valley now on level road. Follow the signs to Grange on the B5277. Less than 2 miles from the A590 is **Grange-over-Sands.** Lunch options include the opulent Netherwood Hotel and the Grange Hotel. Simpler fare can be found at several locations in the town center, which is quite picturesque. Grange is a very pleasant place to take a break. There is a duck pond right on the main street, and a very well-stocked sweet shop that smells heavenly, and where we filled our pockets with toffee. Grange is supposed to have higher temperatures than any other place in the north of England, due to its location between the Lake District hills and the sea. There is a large outdoor swimming pool open during the summer at the west end of the promenade.

Head on through Grange toward Cartmel on the same road after enjoying the many fine scenes here. Grange has been called the Cumbrian Riviera, lying as it does at the north end

of Morecambe Bay. Many hotels and luxury residences line
the coast here, whose views you can enjoy as you climb out
of town on a slight uphill incline. The road turns and dips
into the outlying village.

**Watch for your right turn to Cartmel about 3 miles outside
Grange.** You'll pedal uphill through the stone houses of Alth-
waite, then quickly out into pastures and low hills.

Follow the signs to Cartmel. A mellow downhill takes you the
1¾ miles into **Cartmel.**

Turn right at the X intersection toward Newby Bridge.
Winding through the narrow streets of this fine village, home
of an interesting twelfth-century priory, you quickly enter
farmlands again with bluffs on either side. Large fine manor
homes appear, set back from the road.

Take the left fork a mile out of Cartmel toward Newby Bridge.
You can peek over the hedgerows to view large homes in the
midst of deep fields. You'll see a good-sized church on your
right and several large farms before the road narrows. The
hedges rise higher, and so does the road, on a slight incline.
More fragrant forest encroaches on the road as you roll over
little hills and along the ridge toward the south end of Lake
Windermere.

**Take the left on the A590 toward Newby Bridge after almost
4 miles.** Less than 1 mile brings you into **Newby Bridge.**

Take the right to Hawkshead (not the A592).

Take the fork with the sign to Lakeside Steamers. This road
skirts the west side of Lake Windermere, and we suggest it
as less traveled. You have several opportunities to turn
toward the lakeside. Your route undulates over small hills and
past cottages and fern-bedecked stone walls. You'll catch your
first glimpses of the lake that's been inspiring poets and others
for many years.

Take the right fork after about 2 miles toward Hawkshead. Much of your passage moves through forest and field with intermittent views of the water. The road itself is very beautiful, with rhododendrons and high hedges.

After 2 miles, take the right fork toward Sawrey. This turn keeps you closer to the lake and winds downhill through a glorious forest carpeted with ferns. The downhill is steep, with switchbacks (you'll probably rejoice that you're coming this direction). The lake is visible through the trees. A meadow with grazing sheep introduces another forest and small village. An old farm lies in view of the lake where you also have an unimpeded view of the boats skimming its surface. You pass some hills briefly as you continue winding along the lakeside, and you'll come through a group of houses.

Turn left here toward Sawrey and Hawkshead after about 2½ miles. We had been advised to avoid Windermere itself because of its heavy concentration of cars and tour buses. If you want to visit, you might enjoy parking your bike and taking the ferry here.

Just after turning you have a couple of short, steep climbs, cresting into green pastures and the charming village of **Sawrey,** where we saw people strolling and enjoying the countryside.

Follow the left fork to Hawkshead. Hawkshead is one of the most pleasant spots in the Lake District, well worth a rest stop and a stroll around its quiet pathways. This village was founded in the tenth century, and has the subtle feel that a thousand years of history can give a place. You can visit the grammar school where William Wordsworth was educated and you can see the desk where he carved his name.

Just past **Hawkshead** is a museum in a fifteenth-century courthouse; it is a museum of local rural life and illustrates the history of Hawkshead. A pretty little lake appears shortly before entering Hawkshead, where ducks and sheep roam. Continue following the signs into Hawkshead and Hawkshead village.

Take the fork to Ambleside. The road to Ambleside takes you through very charming territory, over small hills bordered with stone, fern, and forest. There are some hotels where afternoon refueling can be accomplished at outdoor tables, and moor-line landscape in places, with heathery moss and thick undergrowth. A stretch of open country with rock out-croppings leads you up into the shade of large trees and into a gentle up and down stretch. Rhododendrons grace the road-side again as you turn past a particularly pretty meadow. A lovely stream comes into view as you finish the last of the 3¾ miles into **Ambleside.**

Follow the signs to Ambleside on your right.

Follow the signs to Town Centre.

WHERE TO STAY AND DINE IN AMBLESIDE

There is a shortage of budget accommodations in this area, it's being one of the most-visited parts of Britain. We don't have any recommendations here in the Modest range, although you might be able to find them if you have time to look along some of the back lanes of town.

The Salutation Hotel (Ambleside, Cumbria LA22 9BX; tel. [05394]32244) overlooks the town center. It has a pleasant dining room with a timbered and floral decor throughout (Medium–Top)

A personal favorite of ours is the Riverside Hotel, near Rothay bridge (Ambleside, Cumbria LA22 9LF; tel. [05394]32395). This hotel is in a secluded riverside setting slightly out of the town center; all rooms have private bath and color TV. (Top)

The splurge choice here is the Rothay Manor (Rothay Bridge, Ambleside, Cumbria LA22 0EH; tel [05394]33605). The fourteen exquisitely decorated rooms all come with bath, and the whole establishment, especially the renowned kitchen, has a decidedly French air. The lovely setting and thoughtful service are part of the ambience here. You can come here for dinner alone, but be sure to make reservations. (Top)

There are quite a few B&Bs on the main road coming into town, but these can be noisy.

Ambleside is a center of ecological consciousness, so it is possible to get healthy, modern fare in addition to the stodgy British cuisine.

Our favorite place to eat in Ambleside is the Harvest, a fully licensed (meaning they serve alcohol) vegetarian restaurant with an extensive menu, including some unusual vegetarian pâtés, fresh soups, quiches, and vegetarian casseroles. The restaurant is light and equipped with pleasant wooden tables and chairs. (Moderate–Medium)

Just up the street you'll find Zefferelli's Garden Room Café, where you can have a variety of light fare in an ambience of cushioned bamboo chairs and classical music. We feasted there on cappuccino and sticky toffee pudding, which was as deliciously rich as the name implies, smothered in hot fudge sauce and cream. (Moderate–Medium)

WHAT TO SEE AND DO IN AND AROUND AMBLESIDE

The main attraction here is nature. Most people who come to Ambleside do so to hike and enjoy the exquisite beauty of its natural setting. Doll fanciers might enjoy a visit to the new Doll's House Museum, and a side trip can be made to nearby Waterhead to see the excavations of an old Roman site dating from A.D. 79. Probably, though, you'll be most drawn toward the quiet ambience of the wooded areas around town where within a few minutes' walk you can forget the twentieth century and amble along the same trails that inspired Wordsworth.

DAILY SUMMARY

THE LAKE DISTRICT TOUR

Day One: Kendal to Ambleside

(34 miles; moderate to challenging)

- Leave Kendal from the tourist office, heading out on Lowther Street (sign: Hospital).
- After ¼ mile, turn right (sign: Crosthwaite).
- Approximately 2½ miles brings you into Underbarrow.
- After another 1½ miles you enter Crosthwaite.
- Take the right fork here toward Bowness.
- Turn at the left fork in town (sign: Bowland Bridge).
- After a short climb, turn left (signs: Lyth Valley, Grange).
- In under 2 miles, turn right at the stop sign (sign: Cartmel).
- After about a mile, take a right (sign: Cartmel).
- In another 1½ miles, go left (sign: Witherslack).
- After less than a mile, turn left at the fork (sign: Witherslack).
- You'll ride through Witherslack in about 2 miles.
- Turn right here on the busy A590 (signs: Grange, Newby Bridge).
- At the next roundabout in 1 mile, turn on the B5277 (sign: Grange).
- Grange (and lunch) is less than 2 miles. Stay on the main road.
- About 3 miles outside Grange, turn right toward Cartmel and follow the signs to Cartmel for ¾ mile.
- Turn right at the X intersection (sign: Newby Bridge)
- After almost 4 miles, take a left on A590 (sign: Newby Bridge).
- In Newby Bridge after less than 1 mile, turn right toward Hawkshead.
- Take the fork with the sign to lakeside steamers.
- After 2 miles, turn on the right fork (sign: Hawkshead).
- After another 2 miles, turn on the right fork (sign: Sawrey).
- In another 2½ miles, turn left (signs: Sawrey, Hawkshead).
- In Sawrey, follow the left fork to Hawkshead.
- In Hawkshead, a little over 2 miles from Sawrey, take the fork toward Ambleside, which is another 3¾ miles.

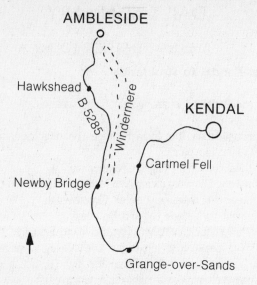

DAY TWO: AMBLESIDE TO ESKDALE GREEN

(36 miles; moderate, with two extremely challenging hills)
In today's 36-mile tour our aim is to take you out of the
condensed area of the Lake District proper for a visit to the
wild backcountry before looping back to the lakes again. Be
forewarned that today's afternoon route contains two very
challenging hills. Other than these puffer hills, the remainder
of the day is moderately hilly. You'll end the day in the very
restful spot of Eskdale Green.

Leave town on the A593 toward Coniston. This may involve
riding around the town center. Eventually you take the signs
past the Rothay Manor and over the bridge past an especially
velvety meadow.

Take the right fork toward Coniston about ½ mile out of town.
The very first part of your ride, which shouldn't be too
crowded if you start early in the morning, follows the musical

bubbling of the stream and passes a little stone bridge over the water. You'll climb a short mild rise and turn into a valley where a couple of hotels have wisely decided to locate. The waterside road makes its ribboned way over short elevations and around ridges defined by gray stone walls.

Take the left fork toward Coniston after 2 miles. A steep uphill leads you up for about a mile, passing lovely tableaus of cottages and gardens, before turning downhill with a magnificent view of the Furness Fells to the right. Another climb, moderate to steep, leaves this view and rises for another mile or so with the mountains accompanying your steep descent into woodland meadows and a small pool. This stretch of road is fully magnificent, a medley of thick meadows, craggy bluffs, and tall pines and plump trees of many varieties. Follow the main road toward Coniston, which passes several tempting farmhouse B&Bs. Public footpaths abound in this area, and we saw people removing their hiking boots after some vigorous meandering. The road is more level now, with an occasional hiccup of a hill. The house density increases as you approach Coniston.

After 5 miles, take the left fork toward Hawkshead. The stream follows the road here.

Turn left after a few hundred yards through the valley. You'll see Coniston Water on your right.

Take the right fork here that says East of Lake. After a few hundred yards following the edge of the water, the road rises sharply past several great B&Bs and rides the ridge with superb views of the water below. The road rises and falls over gentle hills, then descends through thick forest to parallel the water only 100 feet away. One thing you will not see on this pristine road is trash; the visitors seem truly to respect the countryside. We saw many cyclists on this route, most on mountain bikes and many with children. The narrow road continues up and down dale, sometimes no farther than 50 feet from the water, and often past heavy fern outcroppings.

Little hillocks of trees frame the water, where the rocky beach provides a launching place for small boats, fishermen, and windsurfers. Meadows appear toward the south end of the lake, and some especially huge trees and rhododendron bushes provide a deep shade. You'll come past a few clustered houses as the road moves beyond the lake through valley land and pastures. Continue on the main road. The lakeside stretch of road has covered 9 miles.

Turn right toward Newby Bridge, then take a quick left onto the A5084. This wider road heads up and down moderate hills for almost a mile.

Take a sharp right onto the A5092. This road rolls up and down moderate hills at the end of the valley. A fairly steep hill after a couple of miles leads into **Cawthwaite,** a postage stamp village, and continues up steeply for a little over a mile. You're in Moorish land now, with short grasses on the sprawling hills. You'll come in the sweeping panorama and downhill after 2 miles. You'll cover territory fast on this blazing downhill that passes through **Grizebeck** and swings briefly uphill again. Another downhill, more moderate, leads into low-lying pastureland with a meadering stream through the middle. Flattening out, the pavement rolls along for about a mile.

3½ miles from Cawthwaite, turn left and uphill toward Broughton. After a short rise the pathway descends through switchbacks into the rural village of **Broughton** for lunch. The Old King's Head is a local pub. Off the square in the center of town is the popular Square Café, which is open all day. Broughton is a busy little market town that has a church which dates from the eleventh century. You might also enjoy a pause at the Broughton Tower and its dungeons, at the north end of town. There is also a motorcycle museum here.

After lunch, turn left at the sign to Ulpha.

Just out of town take the right turn at the roundabout toward Ulpha.

About a mile from town, turn right toward Ulpha. You'll burn off your lunch on this initially steep climb through heavy ferns and trees. (This is one of the two big afternoon climbs we mentioned.) You'll crest in a little over ½ mile and view a long panorama up the valley. You'll continue over short hills as you progress up the valley on the side of the hill. The countryside has a highlands look, with fern-covered hillsides under gray rock strata. The air has a high mountain freshness. The river is an ideal place to stop; rest your legs by the bubbling water. The road heads uphill through wild-feeling terrain where adventurous sheep wandered onto the road.

4 miles from Broughton, turn right, toward Eskdale.

After less than ½ mile turn left toward Eskdale.

An extremely steep uphill climbs in switchbacks for over ¼ mile. You may have to walk your bike on this short, but epic, hill (the second afternoon thrill). After another mile or so another moderate uphill takes you over stream-rich grassland, dotted with rocks and fat tufts of grass.

Take the right fork toward Eskdale. Up here they don't even fence the sheep. The vista is miles long up into the Cumbrian Mountains. You'll thrill to a wild, careening downhill after 1½ miles, descending out of the highlands into a part of the Lake District that few tourists ever see, a Shangri-la Valley of great beauty. One more short hill takes you into the valley.

Continue on the road to Eskdale. A curving road takes you through the basically level route the 1 mile into **Eskdale.**

Go left at the intersection toward Holmrook. A moderate up-and downhill takes you past great hiking trails and the old stone houses of this village.

This idyllic spot is about as far away from the Lake District tourist bustle as you can get. It really does seem as if you're stepping into an earlier time. We recommend spending the night here purely because we found it enlivening to soak up the feeling of what this territory was like before the tour buses arrived. The chief attraction here is the land itself. The village of Eskdale Green makes a perfect base camp for exploring the valley and surrounding fells. There are supposedly many prehistoric cairns scattered through these hills, although we were not able to find any ourselves. If you are interested in ancient Britain, you can hire a guide to the area.

WHERE TO STAY AND DINE IN ESKDALE

There is one fine place to stay here, and you will need to book ahead to reserve it. The old stone-built Bower House Inn (Eskdale, Holmrook, Cumbria CA19 1TD; tel [09403]244) stands next to the village cricket grounds. The inn will add to your feeling that you are stepping back into another time, but each room comes with a completely modern bathroom and TV. (Medium)

You'll find hounds to be a major topic of conversation here among the locals. Indeed, we may say with certainty that we learned more about hounds in the Lake District than we ever imagined. We spent part of a quiet Sunday afternoon watching a local cricket match here, but came no closer to understanding this quintessential English pastime.

DAILY SUMMARY

THE LAKE DISTRICT TOUR

Day Two: Ambleside to Eskdale Green

(36 miles; moderate, with two extremely challenging hills)

• Leave Ambleside on the A593 (sign: Coniston).
• About ½ mile out of town, turn on the right fork toward Coniston.
• In 2 miles, take the left fork toward Coniston.

- After 5 miles, turn at the left fork toward Hawkshead.
- Turn left after a few hundred yards through the valley.
- Take the right fork here (sign: East of Lake)
- In 9 miles, turn right toward Newby Bridge, then a quick left on the A5084.
- In less than a mile, turn sharply right on the A5092.
- About 2 miles takes you into Cawthwaite.
- Another 2 miles brings you through Grizebeck.
- 3½ miles from Cawthwaite, turn left (sign: Broughton).
- In Broughton, turn left at the sign to Ulpha.
- Stay on the roads toward Ulpha at the roundabout just out of town and again after a mile.
- 4 miles from Broughton, turn right (sign: Eskdale).
- In less than ½ mile, take the left turn (sign: Eskdale).
- This extremely steep hill climbs in switchbacks for over ¼ mile.
- Take the right fork toward Eskdale.
- Stay on the road toward Eskdale for the next 2½ miles.

DAY THREE: ESKDALE TO BUTTERMERE

(33 miles; moderate, with a few challenging hills)
Today you'll experience the contrasts of the Cumbrian area, from highlands to cosmopolitan center to majestic lakes and

fells. Most of your 33-mile ride is moderate, with a few challenging climbs, especially in the morning. You'll stop for the night at a jewel of a village.

Just past the inn, take the right fork toward Gosforth. You begin the day with another stimulating climb to help you work off the English breakfast you just consumed. You level out after ½ mile and cycle through fields with the hills rising to the right. This rolling hill country bends through evergreen brush and tall trees, then downhill.

After 2 miles, take the right fork toward Gosforth by the stream. A steady, gentle uphill snakes through hedgerows and the smell of hay.

Take the *right* fork, not the left, to Holmrook. The road here is fairly level between high hedgerows. You'll glimpse rich fields and tree windbreaks beyond. Many public footpaths take off across the fields. You cross the stream and pass the trimmed hedges of homes with large rhododendrons blooming profusely in summer. After 4½ miles you arrive in **Gosforth.** An uphill takes you through town.

Take the A595 right toward Workinghaven. This wider thoroughfare covers gentle hills through the small village of **New Mill,** then winds over open pastureland, with the sea visible to the left. Almost 3 miles brings you to **Calderbridge.**

Turn right toward Ennerdale. You're back on the small rural road now, into sweeping fields.

After about a mile, turn left toward Ennerdale Bridge, then make a quick right, following the signs to Ennerdale. A moderate uphill comes out into the rolling farmlands of rural northeast England. Wildflowers spring up in the hedges. A downhill rolls into a gentle upgrade, then a moderate hill for about a mile. Follow another gentle hill up, over and down.

At its base take the main road toward Ennerdale Bridge. You're cycling uphill on a steady grade through land where sheep dominate the territory. A rare stand of pines lies along the hills of this wild land. The route is uphill for almost 3 miles, then begins to roll more downhill, with one more short uphill. Some houses appear in the distance, the first signs of civilization for miles.

4 miles from your last turnoff, you take a right toward Ennerdale and Cockermouth. There is one large hotel with a dining room in **Ennerdale** and a couple of smaller places for lunch here after your morning climb.

Take the left fork toward Cockermouth. The road out of town—you guessed it—rises moderately for a little over a mile, then levels out through the village. A short hill takes you into rural terrain with hedges and fences checkerboarding the fields.

After 2 miles, at the T intersection, take the right on A5086 toward Cockermouth. This wider road winds over the gentle and moderate hills. You'll stay on the A5086 for 8 miles. As you approach Cockermouth you'll see the famous peaks of the Cumbrian Mountains off to the right. The fields and widely placed farms contribute to the feeling of space and peace in this part of your ride.

Follow the signs left and quickly right toward Cockermouth. After a mile you come into **Cockermouth.** Follow the signs down into the town center. Cockermouth has more of interest than merely an unusual name. It's been a market town of the region since 1221, and is the birthplace of a number of famous people, including William Wordsworth. Its castle was built in the twelfth century to help the English keep the marauding Scotsmen at bay, and one wing is still in use as a private residence.

Turn right in the town center toward Lorton.

After a few blocks turn left on the B5292 toward Lorton and Buttermere.

Take the right fork, after 2 more blocks, toward Lorton on the B5292. The initial uphill takes you under the A66. The low hills are leading back toward the lakes again.

Follow the sign to Lorton.

After 2 miles, take the right fork toward Buttermere. This leads you immediately through **Lorton,** a small village in a beautiful setting. You come out of the village into very high hedgerows for a short distance. The vistas that appear next are inspiring, and in fact have been the inspiration for much poetry, painting, and music through the years. The fences high up the hills are fascinating reminders of the fell farming of the region.

Turn left after 2½ miles toward Buttermere and Crummock Water. This fork takes you on a gentle upward incline by the stream and through mossy trees up into fields nestled against the high fells. Cresting the small hill after a little over a mile, you roll over into a spectacular view of Crummock Water. Some moderate but short hills lead generally downward beside the water with the mountains rising all around. Mountain streams feed into the lake at several points, and the green and gray hues of the mountains lend a solemn majesty to this region. This is just as beautiful as Lake Windermere without all the crowds. Your view of the lake is unimpeded all the way along its long banks. Then the road passes into a burst of trees at the end of the lake on an uphill slope with level patches for the last mile into **Buttermere.**

WHERE TO STAY AND DINE IN BUTTERMERE

Buttermere is most renowned for its severe beauty and abundance of nature walks. Power boats are not allowed on the water, which is largely owned by the National Trust, but you can rent a rowboat. Situated between Crummock Water and Buttermere Lake, it has several charming B&Bs and a hotel, the Bridge Hotel (Buttermere, Cumbria, CA13 9UZ; tel. [059685]252 or 266), a two-star establishment built of stone, with comfortable public rooms, a good, varied dining menu, and spacious bedrooms. (Top)

At the other end of the tariff spectrum, Cragg Farm (Buttermere, Cockermouth, Cumbria, CA13 9XA; tel. [059685]204) is a pleasant little B&B, just as you come into the village. (Modest)

About a mile past the village of Buttermere, on Buttermere Lake, is another excellent choice for tonight's lodging. The Dalegarth Guest House (Buttermere, Cockermouth, Cumbria, CA13 9XA; tel. [059685]233), surrounded by flowering rhododendrons, with walks by the lake, serves both dinner and breakfast. (Modest)

From the vantage point of this village, the grandeur of the Cumbrian hills is evident every way you look. Dozens of walks, both easy and difficult, crisscross this wild country, much of which is owned by the National Trust and will therefore remain undeveloped. About two hundred years ago this village was the scene of a great national stir when a woman named Mary Robinson, known as the "Beauty of Buttermere," was married with great fanfare to a man posing as a nobleman. After a while, however, the "nobleman" was discovered to be a forger and all-around scoundrel. He was hanged a year later. The big attraction here is wild nature, and comfortable talks around the fire at night with the other ourdoor types who are drawn to this area. This is not the tourist Lake District; this is the real thing, savored by the locals.

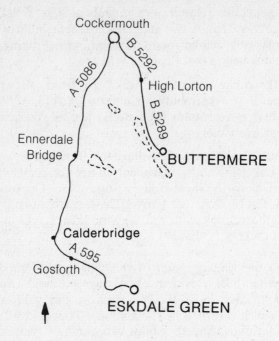

DAILY SUMMARY

THE LAKE DISTRICT TOUR

Day Three: Eskdale to Buttermere

(33 miles; moderate, with a few challenging hills)

- Just past the inn in Eskdale, take the right fork toward Gosforth.
- In 2 miles, turn on the right fork (sign: Gosforth).
- Take the right fork to Holmrook.
- You'll reach Gosforth in 4½ miles, where you turn on the A595 (sign: Workinghaven).
- Passing through New Mill, you come into Calderbridge in almost 3 miles.
- Turn right here toward Ennerdale.
- In 1 mile, turn left, then quickly right, toward Ennerdale.
- After another mile, take the main road toward Ennerdale Bridge.

- 4 miles from the last turn, take a right toward Ennerdale and Cockermouth.
- In Ennerdale, take the left fork toward Cockermouth.
- After 2 miles, turn right on A5086 (sign: Cockermouth).
- In Cockermouth, after another mile, follow the signs through town center.
- Turn right in town center toward Lorton.
- In a few blocks go left on B5292 (signs: Lorton, Buttermere).
- Follow the sign to Lorton.
- In 2 miles, take the right fork toward Buttermere, which leads immediately through Lorton.
- After 2½ miles, turn left toward Buttermere and Crummock Water.
- Buttermere is 10½ miles from Cockermouth.

DAY FOUR: BUTTERMERE TO GRASMERE

(25 miles; moderate, with a few challenging sections)
Today you'll ride from beautiful to heavenly, from majestic to awesome, through what some people consider the most lovely stretch of countryside in England. You'll ride a moderate to challenging pass in the morning, so we are keeping your mileage low today, approximately 25 miles. Your evening stop is our favorite village in this area. We're sure you'll create many memories of your own to treasure.

Leave Buttermere on the main road. (sign: Keswick via Honister Pass) The road first descends toward the deep blue-green water of Lake Buttermere. Sheep take their own tours beside the road. Tree groves stand between the road and the water in sections. There are several places to stop and enjoy the serenity of the water. At the end of the lake the road takes a steep downhill over a stream and begins moving through the wild highlands. Here a stream gurgles at your left as the fells rise steeply on either side. About 3 miles into your ride the road begins ascending, gently at first, but you'll see your route rising before you. Boulders and rock heaps are scattered over the hillside, and your uphill becomes challenging in short bursts. You may feel the need to walk your bike for ¼ mile or so. You'll see the natural source of the stone walls here as you crest the pass after a breathless mile. Your downhill thankfully begins here and bends through the initial moderate downhill. You'll see a sign here that says "Pedal Cyclists Strongly Advised to Walk," so be advised. In fact, if your brakes are not excellent, this is a good recommendation. You'll hear and see a beautiful little stream with ferns and trees enjoying its sustenance. A small village is gathered at the base of the pass.

Stay on the main road here to your left.

Take the left fork after ½ mile toward Keswick. Stone walls and cliffs intermingle with deep meadows as you ride through the small village of **Rossthwaite,** with a general store where you can purchase a drink or other supplies. There are several hotels where morning tea or coffee is served. We saw many well-equipped hikers in this area, renowned for its trails. The hills here are forest-lined, and the road is very winding, with gentle hills by the stream. You're heading uphill again with level recovery areas. About ¾ mile south of Grange you'll see the Bowder Stone, an Ice Age leftover which is the largest boulder in the Lake District. You'll pass a left fork where you can detour to visit the interesting village of Grange, once owned by monks. The road rises over a hill to enter the south end of Derwent Water, considered one of the most beautiful lakes in the district. You're still heading uphill gently and moderately, through thick foliage and stone walls bordering the lake. You'll see a couple of little islands in the middle of the lake. Meadows appear among the thick groves, and a walking path to the left of the road. Finally, 6½ miles from your last fork you come into **Keswick,** your well-earned lunch stop.

Keswick is an interesting place to visit in its own right. Very much a capital city of Lake District hiking and now mountain biking, you will find lots of healthy-looking people striding the streets. If you decide to pause here for a look around, there is a stone circle on a hill east of town. Known as the Castlerigg Circle, it has sixty stones and was apparently built around 1400 B.C. Just as you come into town, you'll see the Lakeside Car Park. There is a charming tea garden here with a fine view of the lake. There is also a pleasant nature walk called the Friar's Crag Walk along the eastern shore of the lake. Here the critic John Ruskin said that the view from the crag was one of the three most beautiful sights in Europe. See if you agree. The town center is loaded with pubs and hotels. A large bakery and confectionary is available for your glucose needs.

Leave Keswick on the A591 toward Windermere. A row of houses ushers you from town, with the river running to your left.

After a short rise a little less than a mile from town, turn right on the A591 toward Windermere. The road continues to rise steadily on moderate incline and leaves the busy feel of the town. You'll crest after a mile or so on this spacious thorough-fare that is the only route down to Grasmere. A long, rolling downhill brings you into camping territory and past regularly spaced farmhouses. The road, which becomes a dual carriage-way for a short interval, is heading downhill or flat, with occa-sional small hills.

Continue on the A591. Look up to the left and see the water-fall coming down through the fells. You encounter a short hill and see Thirlmere rippling to your right. Trees grow right down to the shores on both sides, and the air has the heady combination of forest and wet musk. At the end of the lake the road rises on a steady incline through close-growing grass and stones for $2/3$ mile, then rolls into a treeless section of road between valleys. You'll see one of our favorite areas and the site of a breakfast of field mushrooms that we're still discussing eight years later. Just on the outskirts of **Grasmere,** the view from the Bramrigge B&B (tel. Grasmere 360), run by Major and Mrs. M. E. Fisher, in our Modest range, is a stunning combination of valley and stony fell.

WHERE TO STAY AND DINE IN GRASMERE

Welcome to Grasmere, home of William Wordsworth during the most productive phase of his career. You can visit his burial site in the churchyard here. Wordsworth said that Grasmere was "the loveliest spot that man hath ever found." We would agree. There is something undeniably special about the feeling of this village and environs. Besides Wordsworth, Grasmere is also known for its famous gingerbread, the recipe for which is considered so secret that it's kept in a bank vault.

There is no shortage of fine lodging and even finer dining in this quiet village. There are two small hotels just as you come into the village on the left that we can highly recommend.

The Grasmere Hotel (Broadgate, Grasmere, Cumbria, LA22 9TA; tel [09665]277) is the labor of love of Ian and Annette Mansie, and has everything you would want in a country hotel. Its twelve bedrooms are all named after poets and local characters. The Grasmere has *cordon bleu* dining on unusual dishes such as carrot and coriander soup and red mullet *en papilotte*. The desserts here are also innovative, including Grand Marnier soufflé and hazelnut strawberry pavlova. (Medium–Top)

Right next door, the Oak Bank Hotel (Grasmere, Cumbria, LA22 9TA; tel. [09665]297) has fourteen rooms and serves a five-course gourmet dinner in the evenings. (Medium–Top)

The splurge option in town is the grand Wordsworth Hotel (Grasmere, Ambleside, Cumbria, LA22 9SW; tel. [09665]592), which has thirty-five gorgeously appointed bedrooms and comes complete with an indoor heated swimming pool, sauna, and mini gym. Its dining room and lounge look like an English garden. (Top).

DAILY SUMMARY

THE LAKE DISTRICT TOUR

Day Four: Buttermere to Grasmere

(25 miles; moderate, with a few challenging sections)

- Leave Buttermere on the main road (sign: Keswick via Honister Pass).
- The road ascends after 3 miles for 1 mile, then heads steeply downhill.
- Stay on the main road to your left at the base.
- After ½ mile, turn left (sign: Keswick).
- After 6½ miles you'll enter Keswick.
- Exit Keswick on A591 (sign: Windermere).
- In less than 1 mile, turn right to stay on A591 (sign: Windermere).
- The A591 takes you the 13 miles into Grasmere.

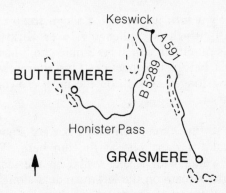

DAY FIVE: GRASMERE TO CALDBECK

(40 miles; moderate to challenging)
This is a strenuous day, full of many challenges and beauty. If you want a last look at the central lakes, you could take the A591 straight down into Kendal and take the train from Oxenholme. This longer (approximately 40-mile) day has several climbs, one over a steep pass just after Ambleside, and

passes the lovely lake of Ullswater before turning toward the very northern end of the park.

Leave Grasmere on the A591 toward Windermere. You'll pass the lovely little Grasmere Lake before heading slightly uphill through light forest and somewhat lower fells. You'll pass many tempting guest houses and B&Bs through **Rydal,** about 2½ miles from Grasmere, Wordworth's home in his last years and famous for its sheep dog events in the fall. You'll then head through some of the more heavily trafficked sections in this region. A morning start should save you a crush. About 3 miles from Grasmere you reenter **Ambleside,** for a pass-through.

Follow the A591 through the familiar town center.

Turn left on the North Road in front of the Salutation Hotel.

Take the right fork up the hill, a short, steep climb. Continue up the hill, which is challenging, over Kirkstone Pass with stone walls on either side. This 3-mile climb has another steep section just before the junction. Our alternative to this challenge was a long excursion on the most crowded road in the Lake District.

Turn left at the summit on A592 toward Penrith. You may want to take a short rest at the inn here. The road turns steeply downhill with a lake visible in the distance. As you descend, the stream on the left meanders along with the curving road. A series of short, small hills takes you through the fells and around to the lake. Wildflowers, ferns and trees line the lake.

Stay on the road toward Patterdale (A592). The road crosses the water, which runs in a stream to your right now, as the road brushes by water-rich ferns and flows over these slight hills and by an ancient stone barn. You have descended 4 miles from the summit when you pass through **Patterdale,** whose enviable setting is replete with large trees and rich meadows. There are a couple of hotels here that we suggest you explore for their gustatory possibilities and also a very pretty church. **Glenridding** follows on Patterdale's heels, and is right on the shore of Ullswater. Boats are moored at the harbor, and you can stop for a cruise on the lake. Rhododendrons add to the festive air of this resort village. The small hills continue as you pedal through mossy rock outcroppings, your path outlining the lake's edge. The fells visibly form a bowl where the surrounding streams feed into the lake. This long lake has many wonderful views, both of water and of the supporting cast of meadows and hills. Then, 7 miles from Patterdale, you ride into **Watermillock,** a small village of cultivated lawns and charming B&Bs with views of the water.

A mile past the village turn left toward Penruddock. We want to avoid the bustle of Penrith and take you around on back roads to Carlisle. The road is moderately uphill for a little over a mile after your turn, heading up into the fells. On this trip we saws B&Bs everywhere, some on this road.

Take the left fork, which is a quite challenging uphill for ⅓ mile. After you crest the hill, your downhill runs moderately and steeply through rural land where sheep abound. Follow the signs to Penruddock.

Turn right at the T fork (unmarked in this direction).

Cross the A66 on the B5288 toward Greystoke, 6 miles from Watermillock.

Take the right turn on B5288 toward Greystoke. Keep following the signs toward Greystoke over this cultivated and tidy area of hedged fields and cattle pastures. The road, blessedly, is fairly level here. After 3 miles you come through **Greystoke**.

At the X intersection take the road straight through toward Jonby and Blencow.

Go right at the fork toward Blencow and Carlisle. Greystoke
is best known for its church, one of the largest in the area,
and its medieval sanctuary stone. As you exit this little village
of ancient stone, you'll get another wide view of the lovely
valley between hedgerows. There are some surprising and attractive homes out here.

In **Blencow**, take the left road toward Carlisle.

At the next intersection go toward Hutton-in-the-Forest. A
light hill on this wider road leads into a deeply green area of
graceful lines of trees and neat hedges enclosing the fields.

In the humorously named village of **Unthank**, after 2 miles,
turn left on the B5305 toward Sebergham. You're on fairly
level roads through working farms and long-standing tree
windbreaks. After about 1½ miles you have a slight rise to
climb for about ½ mile. Stay on the main road here, over
long rolling hills. You'll cycle past several well-tended houses
of stone.

Turn left toward Hesket Newmarket after 4 miles on the
B5305.

Follow the signs over hill and dale toward Caldbeck. The final
miles into Caldbeck run through very lush riverside trees and
fields. Caldbeck is located at the north end of the Lake District National Forest, and has the wonderful green surroundings characteristic of the region. You pass first through **Hesket
Newmarket,** then on a road which is consistently hilly with
small elevations. Another 1½ miles brings you into **Caldbeck.**

WHERE TO STAY AND DINE IN CALDBECK

Now you have toured from the farthest south to the farthest
northern part of the Lake District. Caldbeck is an easygoing
place to rest up from the rigors of riding, and it is an easy
ride on into Carlisle, which has good train connections to the
rest of the U.K.

Monoleys (Caldbeck, Cumbria, CA7 8DX; tel. [06998]234 or 367), right in the center of the village, is a clean, surprisingly modern establishment. Their afternoon teas are very nicely done here; in fact, the dining room is a credit to the establishment. (Medium)

A farmhouse B&B nearby is Friar Hall (Caldbeck, Wigton, Cumbria, CA7 8DS; tel ([06998]633) is a quieter option if you want to be a little ways out of the bustle—though there's not much bustle in Caldbeck. You'll experience the real charm of Caldbeck off its main street. Friar Hall is down a lane across from the church by a stream; you reach it by beginning to head out of town on the B5299 toward Carlisle and turning right on Friar's Row. Good walks, great surrounding vistas, and pleasant strolls, especially along Friar's Row, await you. (Modest–Medium)

DAILY SUMMARY

THE LAKE DISTRICT TOUR

Day Five: Grasmere to Caldbeck

(40 miles; moderate to challenging)

- Leave Grasmere on A591 (sign: Windermere).
- You'll pass through Rydal about 2½ miles from Grasmere.
- In another ½ mile, in Ambleside, follow the A591 through town center.
- Turn left on North Road in front of the Salutation Hotel.
- Take the right fork up this short, steep climb, less steeply with one further steep section over its 3-mile rise.
- At the summit, turn left on A592 (sign: Penrith).
- Stay on A592 (sign: Patterdale).
- You'll come into Patterdale 4 miles from the summit, quickly followed by Glenridding.
- 7 miles from Patterdale, Watermillock appears.
- 1 mile past this village, turn left toward Penruddock.
- After a little over 1 mile, take the left fork, and follow the signs to Penruddock.

- Turn right at the T fork (unmarked in this direction).
- 6 miles from Watermillock, cross the A66 on B5288 toward Greystoke.
- Take the right turn on B5288 (sign: Greystoke).
- After 3 miles, in Greystoke, take the road straight through the X intersection toward Honby and Blencow.
- Turn right at the fork (signs: Blencow, Carlisle).
- In Blencow, turn left toward Carlisle.
- At the next intersection, head toward Hutton-in-the-Forest.
- After 2 miles, in Unthank, turn left on B5305 (sign: Sebergham).
- In 4 miles, turn left on B5305 (sign: Hesket Newmarket).
- After Hesket Newmarket, Caldbeck is another 1½ miles.

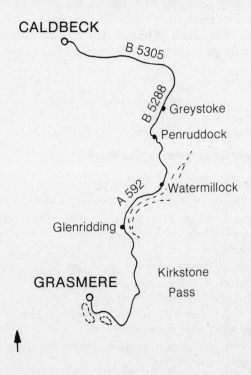

DAY SIX: GETTING TO CARLISLE TO CATCH THE TRAIN

Leave Caldbeck on the B5299 toward Carlisle. Heathery bushes run along the hills on your initial moderate climb of about ½ mile.

Turn right on the B5299 toward Carlisle. A short downhill turns into a longer, easy but steady uphill over the ridge with Carlisle already visible in the distance. You begin descending through tall bushes 3 miles out of town.

Take the B5299 straight across the X intersection toward Carlisle. The road is a gentle rollercoaster here, passing through a little village and leveling out into broad fields. This is a fairly straightforward shot to Carlisle to get you there as quickly as possible while avoiding the more heavily trafficked roads. The rollercoaster ribbon of the center line appears and disappears over the next small hill through landscape that summarizes the past few days.

Keep following the signs to Carlisle, which are clearly marked. You'll come through another, little larger village (**Dalton**).

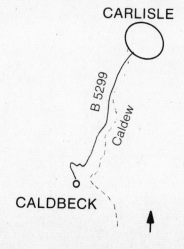

8 miles from Caldbeck, take the left fork toward Carlisle. A sidewalk appears, letting you know you're entering civilization. The population density increases. A pretty red-stone church stands on the right about 3½ miles outside Carlisle proper. You come through a surprising section of open field again on a wide, mostly flat surface. Stay on the main road, which enters **Carlisle** by a Pirelli tire factory. You'll see signs to the railroad station (to the right) as you come to the first big intersection.

WALES:
THE WILD NORTH
COUNTRY

WE FOUND THE ESSENCE OF WALES ONE DAY BY GETTING lost. We had cruised across the border from England on a back road and were looking for a town large enough to have a B&B where we could spend the night. We took a wrong road (not hard to do in Wales, where many of the tiny back roads do not appear on a map), and ended up so far in the middle of nowhere that we didn't even have a guess as to where we were. Around a curve we spotted a farmhouse, with a tiny B&B sign, and pulled in. We were their first customers of the season and were treated like visiting royalty. Mrs. brought us tea and cake, Daughter taught us the rudiments of the Welsh language, and Mr. entertained us with a few wild tales of his countryman Dylan Thomas. He also gave us a hand with lubricating our bikes. Later in the early evening we walked to the local pub for a pint, and spent a pleasant couple of hours chatting and playing darts with a group of miners.

Several things will become apparent when you come into

Wales. First, the signs are often in Welsh as well as English. We gave up on pronouncing anything but the simplest words. For example, one of the first words in Welsh we saw was Cwm. By asking a waitress, we found out it's pronounced like "coom." But soon we were confronted with Aberystwyth, Llanfairynghornwy, and Penrhyndeudræth—and we gave up.

A second thing the cyclist will surely notice is that the finest parts of Wales are stimulating to the thighs as well as the eyes. It happens that the very best of Wales, in our opinion, runs through part of the Snowdonia National Park. There are some challenging hills here, and these two fortyish bikers, veterans though we are, feel no compunction at recommending that you get off and walk a little ways if you have to. In places such as Wales we are especially grateful for the eighteen speeds of our mountain bikes.

A third thing we noticed right away is that the Welsh are passionate about poetry and song. Even though these hardy folks have had an exceptionally bloody history, their national anthem focuses on their poets as well as their warriors. One of the very best things to do in Wales is to visit pubs or other locations where there is traditional Welsh singing going on. In the summer you'll find it everywhere, particularly on the weekends. It is not uncommon, however, to have amateurs burst into song at even the most out-of-the-way pub. It was explained to us by a bartender: "A Welshman drinks, he sings. Simple as that, love."

DAY ONE: RHYL TO RUTHIN

(34 miles; moderate to challenging)

Rhyl (pronounced *rill*), on the north coast of Wales, is our starting point for this tour. It is an easy town to get to by rail, unlike much of northern Wales. It is possible to get a direct train from London's Euston Station. If you miss the direct link, you may need to change trains in Manchester. From London it is about a three-and-a-half-hour train ride.

Rhyl is a seaside resort, complete with amusement parks and saltwater taffy. The new thrill in Rhyl is the Suncentre, the Welsh solution to the uncertain weather in these parts, being a complete indoor beach. A huge building maintained at a constant temperature of 80° F, you can surf in the indoor surfing pool or take a wild ride down the giant 200-foot Dragon Slide. Last time we rode through here, we were seriously tempted to chuck our tour and spend the day inside.

There is a fine castle to visit 4 miles outside Rhyl. Rhuddlan Castle was built in the thirteenth century, strategically placed by the river by Edward I. The castle makes a good day excursion if you're spending a little extra time in Rhyl.

If you want a good seaside lodging. The Beechroyde Guesthouse (27 Palce Avenue, Rhyl LL18 1HS; tel [0745]350159) is comfortable and close to all the sights of Rhyl. There are scores of B&Bs here, many along the beachfront, and the tourist information office is very helpful. You pay for the back-roads beauty of this region with your thighs: it's hilly. So for this reason, the mileages on this tour tend to be moderate.

Leave town on High Street in the center of town, which will turn into the A525.

At the lights, take the road up over the bridge. (sign: Rhuddlan, A525)

Stay to the left just over the bridge. This residential area is lined with shops and closely spaced houses. Stay on the main road weaving out of town (Rhuddlan Road). After less than a mile you come into **Rhuddlan,** a suburb of Rhyl.

At the roundabout take the A5151 toward Dyserth. After a couple of miles you will pass a castle on your left. Stop to visit, then continue on the upslope, through grasslands and clusters of houses, the 4 miles from Rhyl to **Dyserth.**

Take the right road toward Cwm before you get to the town center. (The Welsh language tends to look a little short on vowels.)

After ¼ mile, turn left toward Tremeirchion and Cwm.

Take a right at the top of this 2-block hill toward Tremeirchion on Cwm Road. This little lane winds up and down hills, quickly coming through **Cwm.**

   The first classic Welsh vista appears as you come out of the village on the one-lane road. The bay to your right and green rolling hills to the left welcome you to the splendors of Wales. You're taking the high road, the ridge that opens on the whole bay. The road has moderately steep hills and enters deeper forest in sections.

After 3½ miles, take the little road across the busy A55 (to Chest and Conwy) toward Tremeirchion. The main roads in Wales are often not very attractive, but we were amazed at how often just a hundred yards or so off the main roads there were outstanding vistas awaiting us. This lane takes a sharp descent, then curves around through gorgeous green hills and views of the trees gathered in the valley. After a mile you come into **Tremeirchion.**

Take the lane toward Bodfari.

After a mile, take the left road toward Denbigh and Bodfari.

At the next fork, stay on the left road. (Don't take the right fork toward Denbigh.) One hill follows another here, leading you farther into beautiful long views of hedged fields and trees with stone farmhouses and fences from time to time. Another 1½ miles brings you into **Bodfari,** a little village with stone buildings of red brick and white stone.

Take the A451 left toward Mold and Denbigh.

Take another left in a couple of blocks. The high hills to your right have lovely homes perched on them and fields with sheep and cattle. The underlying red soil blends with the vivid green for spectacular effect. The road rises on a gentle to moderate slope past huge old trees and a thick forest on the hills to the right. After 3 miles you enter **Afonwen,** a cluster of houses, before you reenter the valley with fields of sheep and hills thick with trees. The road continues steadily up at a slight incline. You'll pass a craft shop in a lovely stone building to your right about a mile out of town. Another 3 miles takes you past a guesthouse and coffee shop on your left—if you need refueling. The road levels out, then heads on an upward incline again.

After 5 miles turn right toward Cilcain. This back road first leads past a large well-maintained farm, then turns up a hill and over into farmland and forest. The road is hilly through the mile into **Cilcain,** a small village of charming houses.

At the X intersection in town, turn left toward Pantymwyn. You'll pass a combination of ancient and modern homes, then bend out into the countryside. You'll pedal the rare downhill here on a very narrow road steeply diving through beautiful deep forest. Over an old stone bridge you then pedal up a steep hill of about ½ mile into **Pantymwyn.**

At the T fork, head left toward Mold. The road out of town continues uphill. The road levels out and actually heads downhill here, passing several large houses.

Take the right fork toward Mold. Stone walls guard the fields in places, wooden ones, or vines and hedges, in others. You come into a more populated area here and follow the sign into **Mold.**

Take a right at the T and the next right into the town center. There is a particularly fine church dominating the town where we suggest a lunch stop. St. Mary's Parish Church is located on the site of an earlier church built in 1253. The present church was built and paid for by Henry Tudor's mother to celebrate his victory over Richard III in the battle of Bosworth (he became Henry VII as a result). The church is beautiful—not only from the outside. Its interior is decorated with a rich profusion of ornaments, including a fascinating animal frieze. The tourist information center will be happy to provide you with a written guide to a historical walk around Mold.

For lunch, we can recommend the Old Nursery tearoom, which is on the second floor above a great and aromatic bakery. They serve homemade soup, fresh-baked breads, and other goodies. If you're a nonsmoker, the Little Pantry, in an arcade near the tourist center, welcomes you with sandwiches, potatoes, quiche, and pastries.

Leave Mold on the A494 to the right. (sign: Ruthin). A few blocks (uphill, naturally, but not severely) take you out into countryside. The grade does turn moderately steep through the suburbs, then quite steep for almost 2 miles. You'll then welcome a long downhill past the outlying stone houses and pubs and into stunning country and **Loggerheads.** This tiny hamlet has a pub and park just off the road. The road climbs a short hill and levels off by emerald fields and homes high on the hillside. After a little less than 2 miles you pass through the small village of **Llanferres.** The A494 has a broad, marked shoulder that cars respect, so you should have no trouble cycling on the most scenic part of the route, the 6 miles to Ruthin. The farms in Wales are large and clearly hardworking. Much of the hillside is utilized for fields. A couple of miles out of town you encounter another steep hill of approximately ½ mile that crests into the most splendid view of the Ruthin valley. Your legs will rejoice at this long, luxurious downhill with an ancient, moss-covered wall in sections. The downhill takes you 2 miles, then up a short hill and over into **Ruthin.**

WHERE TO STAY AND DINE IN RUTHIN

Ruthin is in the beautiful vale of Clwyd (pronounced *clue-id*) that you saw when you crested the long hill a few miles ago. It has the distinction of being the only town where curfew has been rung nightly since the eleventh century. If you've been braving any of that famous Welsh weather, you may welcome a visit to the heated indoor swimming pool. If you follow the signs to the tourist information center, you'll also find the local crafts center, which has pottery, weaving, candles, and the like, done by local artisans.

The major landmark of the town is Ruthin Castle: originally a medieval castle, it now functions as a luxury hotel. A popular thing to do here is to attend one of the medieval banquets at the hotel, which are held every night except Sunday. If you want to stay at the castle, rooms can be booked by calling [08242]2664. (Medium)

If you're not in the mood for staying at a castle, we can recommend the Coach House Hotel (Park Road, Ruthin, LL15 1LB; tel. [08242]4223). All the rooms come with private bath and television sets. Beds and breakfast for two here are quite reasonable. (Modest–Medium)

With its stream and gardens, the Argoed Guest House (Mwrog Street, Ruthin; tel. [08242]3407) is a timbered house with a good view of the nearby hills.

Both the Coach House and Ruthin Castle have good restaurants, as does The Castle Hotel in St. Peters Square (tel. [08242]2479). Many other less formal opportunities abound, such as fish and chips shops.

DAILY SUMMARY

WALES TOUR

Day One: Rhyl to Ruthin

(34 miles; moderate to challenging)

- Leave Rhyl on High Street in the center of town, which will turn into A525.
- At the lights, take the road up over the bridge (sign: Rhuddlan, A525).
- Stay to the left just over the bridge.
- In less than a mile, in Rhuddlan, take A5151 at the roundabout toward Dyserth.

- After 4 miles, in Dyserth, take the road right toward Cwm, before you get to the town center.
- In ¼ mile, turn left toward Tremeirchion and Cwm.
- Take a right after 2 blocks (signs: Tremeirchion, Cwm Road).
- You'll pass quickly through Cwm.
- In 3½ miles, take the little road across A55 toward Tremeirchion.
- In Tremeirchion, after a mile, take the lane toward Bodfari.
- In 1 mile, take the left road toward Denbigh and Bodfari.
- Stay on the left road at the next fork (don't go toward Denbigh).
- After 1½ miles, in Bodfari, turn left on A451 (signs: Mold, Denbigh).
- Turn left again in a couple of blocks.
- In 3 miles you pass through Afonwen.
- After 5 miles turn right toward Cilcain.
- At the X intersection in town, take a left toward Pantymwyn, which you reach in about a mile.
- Take the right fork here toward Mold.
- Follow the signs into Mold and the town center.
- Exit Mold on A494 to the right (sign: Ruthin).
- In the next 4 miles you pass through Loggerheads and Llanferres on A494.
- After another 2 miles you'll come into Ruthin.

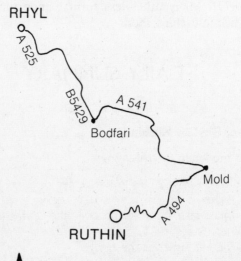

DAY TWO: RUTHIN TO BETWS-Y-CŒD

(34 miles; moderate)
Today you'll be leaving Ruthin, dominated by its medieval castle, with your destination as the fairy-tale village of Betws-y-Cœd (pronounced *bet-us-e-coyd*). Today's 34-mile tour is moderate to challenging.

Leave town at the large roundabout by picking up the A525 toward Denbigh. You have a couple more blocks through town.

Then turn right to follow the A525 and the sign to Denbigh. This relatively flat road runs straight through the outlying houses of Ruthin and the occasional B&B. A short, moderate climb swings over into **Rhewl,** with a beautiful view of the vale of Clwyd back off to the right. The winding pavement is still basically flat for about ½ mile, then climbs again over small hills that curve and reveal more farms and neatly trimmed fields. The 7 miles into Denbigh are uphill at times, but nothing more than moderate. The general inclination is slightly uphill, but you'll find level stretches where you can stretch your legs.

After 4½ miles, at the roundabout, take the left road toward the town center.

Keep following the sign to Town Centre, to the left and uphill. Denbigh has a charming if steep main street, with some tempting opportunities for morning tea. On the Friday we last came through, it was quite bustling. Denbigh Castle is at the top of the hill above the town, reached by turning left at the Bull's Hotel and following the road on up. The castle contains memorabilia from the distinguished local boy, the explorer H. M. Stanley (of "Dr. Livingston, I presume?" fame).

Continue down through town and go left toward Pentre Fœlas.

Up a short hill you encounter another roundabout where you go left toward Nantglyn.

At the unmarked T, turn right.

After a block, turn right on the B4501, (sign: Nantglyn) A short hill rolls over into a narrow lane walled with old stone on a moderate downhill and over an old stone bridge. Passing a few houses, you head steeply for ¼ mile, then more moderately, along deep glades, for another.

Take the left fork to stay on the B4501. Passing a Welsh sheep farm and stone barn, the narrow path continues gently uphill.

Continue on the B4501. A very steep uphill confronts you for about a mile; once over you're into glorious countryside. At the base of the downhill, 3 miles from your turn onto the B4501, you come to an X intersection in the middle of the fields.

Turn right on B5435 toward Bylchau. We didn't encounter a single car on this stretch of road. Your turn takes you on a rollercoaster downhill, under heavy vines and overhanging trees, where it is misty enough to support large ferns. An extremely narrow stone bridge takes you up into a little unmarked village and another X intersection.

Continue across (the sign is around the corner) to stay on the B5435 toward Bylchau. The short uphill takes you past very restful scenery to your right; go up the right fork into more residences perched on the side of the hill, with the valley and left bank beyond. Breaks in the tall bushes reveal a large farmhouse in the valley. We stopped to admire the scene; everywhere around us echoed the sound of sheep bleating on the faraway hills. The gray stone of the farmhouse against a sea of green rolling hills: we thought that this one moment would have made the entire tour worthwhile. The road continues climbing, again very steeply, for a mile.

Turn left on the A543 toward Bylchau. You come into **Bylchau** after less than 1⅓ miles.

Continue to your left on the A543 toward Pentre Fœlas. Some heathery hills appear, with tufts of grass and grazing sheep, as the wider road turns and winds uphill on a moderate grade. You'll see part of the reservoir as you continue on the A543. This more austere section of road passes through grasslands and low hills as far as the eye can see. Another body of water is visible as you continue on the gently curving hills and slopes the 11 miles to Pentre Fœlas. We considered taking you through more back roads but decided to spare you some energy for exploration tonight. About 8 miles into this section of the ride, after you crest the hills and start bending down, trees begin to reappear in the distance, and the golds and oranges blend into green, with the trimmed fields enclosing sheep. We saw more stone walls here than in the first part of this tour.

Turn right on the A5 toward Betws-y-Cœd. You come immediately into the tiny village of **Pentre Fœlas,** then go on into the lush green valleys, streams, and hills of your last 6-mile section for the day. Cycling through ferns and wood glades, you'll be on a slight upgrade. Stop for a moment to watch the stream flowing to your left. We could understand the source of the growth of trees and the outbursts of rhododendrons. The air is especially fragrant with the smell of fresh grass, clean water, and green growing things. This is prime wool territory, and you'll see a sign for a woolen mill, as well as the wonderful Conwy Falls, about 4 miles along the A5. The countryside goes from beautiful to awesome here, with the downhill taking you into low mountains covered with pine trees.

Turn left toward Betws-y-Cœd.

WHERE TO STAY AND DINE IN BETWS-Y-CŒD

This area—the entrance to it, the feel of the countryside, and the architecture—reminded us of a village in the Dordogne area of France. It's a combination of country charm, lushly forested scenery, and fine little places to stay. Just as you come into town you will see a row of B&Bs, one of which we thought quite highly of. It is called the Mælgwyn House, (Betws-y-cœd, LL24 0AC; tel. [06902]252) and is run by a pleasant couple, the Walshes. It caters to nonsmokers. (Medium)

Just up the street you'll find another charmer, the Mount Garmon Hotel (Betws-y-Cœd, Gwynedd LL24 0AN; tel. [06902]335), a small family-run bed and breakfast in a converted Victorian house. They take pride in their meals here, whether you are having an English breakfast or having dinner with the proprietors, Bill and Jean Major. (Medium)

The Royal Oak Hotel is a luxury option right in the center of town (Betws-y-Cœd, Gwynedd LL24 0AY; tel. [06902]219). It features a lovely restaurant, with decor reminiscent of a California fern bar. The hotel has a commanding view of both the village green and the river. (Top)

A seventeenth-century family-run hotel, the Fairy Glen (Betws-y-Cœd, Gwynedd, LL24 0SH; tel. [06902]269) overlooks the River Conwy in a gorgeous setting a mile outside Betws-y-Cœd village. The sound of the river can lull you to sleep. The Fairy Glen is one of this area's bargain lodgings. (Modest)

Dozens of other accommodations can be accessed through the tourist information office.

As we mentioned, the Royal Oak has one of the best meals in town. More casual options ring the village green. There is a pleasant little cafeteria-style dining room right on the village green that served us a tasty baked potato one rainy afternoon.

WHAT TO SEE AND DO IN BETWS-Y-CŒD

There are several places in town that rent mountain bikes. If you didn't bring yours, this would be a great way to explore some of the mountainous countryside that cannot be reached on a thin-tired bike. Some of the other entertainment options here include visits to Swallow Falls and Miners Bridge, 2 miles west of town near the A5. The Conwy Falls is one of the grandest in Wales. There is a salmon leap here to help the fish get upstream. Indoor options include a railway museum and a summer theater. The village itself, though, is the real attraction here. We have never forgotten its timeless feel.

DAILY SUMMARY

WALES TOUR

Day Two: Ruthin to Betws-y-Cœd

(34 miles; moderate)

- Leave Ruthin at the roundabout on A525 (sign: Denbigh).
- Turn right after a few more blocks to stay on A525.
- Passing soon through Rhewl, after 4½ miles, take the left road at the roundabout toward the town center.
- Keep following the signs to Town Centre, to the left and uphill, in Denbigh.
- Continue down through town and go left toward Pentre Fœlas.
- At the next roundabout, turn left toward Nantglyn.
- Turn right at the unmarked T intersection.
- After 1 block, go right on B4501 (sign: Nantglyn).
- In ½ mile, take the left fork to remain on B4501.
- 3 miles from your turn onto B4501, head right on B5435 (sign: Bylchau).
- Stay on B5435 for a little over a mile.
- Turn left on A543 toward Bylchau, which you'll reach in 1⅓ miles.
- Continue to the left on A543 toward Pentre Fœlas for 11 miles.
- Take a right on A5 toward Betws-y-Cœd, which takes you immediately into Pentre Fœlas.
- 6 more miles on A5 takes you to Betws-y-Cœd.
- Turn left to Betws-y-Cœd.

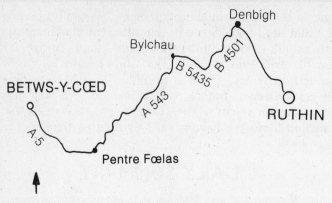

DAY THREE: THE VALE OF CONWY LOOP

A DAY TRIP OPTION

(40 plus miles round trip: moderate)
You might consider spending two nights in Betws-y-Cœd and taking a day trip up the Vale of Conwy to Conwy Bay and back. There are two roads, both of which skirt the Conwy River and lead to the bay. The larger road, more trafficked, is the A470. It lies on the eastern side of the river. You can visit Gwydyr Castle along the way. Another site, Conwy Castle, is quite possibly the most famous of Edward I's network of fortresses in this part of the world. Also along the way is Bodnant Garden, which many horticulture fanciers consider to be one of the finest gardens in the whole U.K. Llandudno, up near Conwy, has two beaches for strolling and a fine promenade, as well as a tramway that is the longest cable car system in Britain and will take you to the summit of Great Orme, where you'll have a great view of the Happy Valley and its environs. You'll be skirting part of the Snowdonia Forest along the way, close enough at times to see and hear the river.

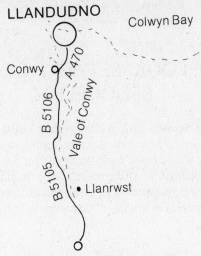

DAILY SUMMARY

WALES TOUR

Day Three: Day Trip Option—Up the Vale of Conwy

(40 plus miles round trip; moderate)

- Past the information center, cross the Waterloo Bridge.
- Take an immediate left on A470 (sign: Conwy).
- After about 3 miles, in Llanrwst, turn left on B5106 (sign: Trefriw). The Forest Visitor Center can be toured just before Llanrwst.
- In Trefriw, head north on B5106 to Tyn-y-groes. *Note:* You can detour here to Llyn Crafnant for a picnic lunch and to Gwydyr Castle.
- In Tyn-y-groes, turn right on A470 (sign: Tal-y-Cafn). Bodnant Garden is approximately 2½ miles on your left.
- After another 2 miles, at the large intersection, follow the signs to Conwy and visit Conwy Castle and Plas Mawr, claimed to be the finest example of Elizabethan town house in Great Britain.
- Ride to Llandudno on the A546 via Degnawy, crossing the road

bridge which is parallel to Telford's suspension bridge. This area is very heavily visited, so be watchful.
• Retrace your route in the afternoon.

DAY FOUR: BETWS-Y-CŒD TO BEDDGELERT

(33 miles; moderate, with a challenging stretch)
The tour today begins and ends in alpine splendor, winding from Betws-y-Cœd for a trek through the Snowdonia Forest, through the beautiful fishing village of Porthmadog, and back into the glorious mountains to Beddgelert. Your 33-mile route is primarily moderate, with a challenging 2-mile stretch over the pass.

Leave Betws-y-Cœd by the A5 going east back out of town.

Take the right fork on A5 and A470 toward Dolgellau.

Take an immediate right on A470 toward Dolgellau. The river flows to your right as you ride along this fairly busy road (there is no other way to go through Snowdonia). You pass a great looking B&B on the right that you might consider for your second night. The beauty of the area will inspire you to keep breathing to accommodate the splendor. After about 3 miles of gentle uphill you come under a stone arched bridge and head more steeply uphill for the next couple of miles. The river roars over large boulders as you rise up out of the valley floor, with the stone wall to your left, and view the forest-covered mountains and ferns on the hills to the right. Another 2 miles brings you past a bridge over the river to the left and on through the stone outcroppings and rich valley meadows. In 6 miles you come into the historic village of **Dolwyddelan.** You can visit the ruins of the twelfth-century castle, visible on the hill just past the village. If you climb up to the castle you can get a good view of the valley below. The road is fairly level here for a short distance, then heads uphill again on a moderate upgrade for a mile, then steeply uphill for another mile. Moss- and heather-covered stone out-croppings erupt from the ground on your right. The landscape has a more desolate look as you continue to climb on a mod-erate, steady uphill with the mountains rolling off in the dis-tance to the right. These mountains look as if they're covered with dense green fur. After 3 miles of climbing, the road crests and begins heading downhill past the world's largest slate mine. Slag heaps cover the hills in chaotic piles. There is a shop here where you can get sandwiches and tea.

Take the right fork on A496 and the next fork to Porthmadog after another mile. The road moves toward the bay with the severe Snowdonia Mountains fading into the distance. The road takes a steep downhill run for ¼ mile or so, then be-comes more level before plunging again through forest and high rock cliffs. These lush but sometimes forbidding high mountains, look like a natural setting for Tolkien's *Lord of the Rings*. This section, swelling with trees and shot through with streams, could have been the taking-off place for the book's expedition. The road is level and rolls through the valley.

3 miles into the valley, turn toward Porthmadog. The road is wider here and you'll see rhododendrons crowding the hillside as the water broadens and becomes placid. A turn brings you into a more slight uphill grade after a mile, with trees looking as if they're about to spill into the road. A steeper short run is your entrance to the houses on the hills of **Penrhyn-deudræth.** It may take you longer to pronounce this name than to ride through this seaside village.

Stay on the A497 toward Porthmadog.

Take a little side trip to the left to visit the Italianate village of Portmeirion. This forest glen road takes you a little over a mile into the viewing area where you can park your bike.

A man named Sir Clough William Ellis had a dream de-cades ago of creating a Mediterranean village such as Portofino. We were looking around the pastels, arches and ornate courtyard of this fantasy village when we noticed that it looked like the set of "The Prisoner" (our younger readers may not remember this classic TV series of the 1960s). When we came back out we inquired at the admissions hut and were told that indeed, the series was filmed here, including the sequences where the prisoner tries to escape across a sandy inlet. There is a "Prisoner" information center and shop here, and the guide said that every year people come for a festival and ride about in little carts and "dress up like the prisoner and dance about and such."

Follow the way out signs to leave Portmeirion back through the forest and meadow.

Turn left at the T junction and glance over to the stone cliffs to the right. Here is where you board the famous Ffestiniog Railway, a narrow-gauge railway which chugs several times a day up into the mountains and back. On nice days the views up and down this track are superlative, sometimes reaching all the way to the mountains of Ireland. For some reason, you have to pay a toll of 5p to get down into **Porthmadog,** where you arrive after 2 miles. This growing seaside resort has one main area with several shops.

Go left on the A487 toward Cærnarfon. This gets you into **Tremadog.**

Take the A487 to the right toward Beddgelert. This spacious road takes you out of the village and back around the high stone cliffs on a valley road, with meadows and pastures and the occasional stone farmhouse. After 2 miles the stone wall now appears on your right as you ride through **Prenteg.**

Keep following the signs to Beddgelert. After another ½ mile the road enters a forested area through a canopy of tall trees and begins to rise over small hills. The cool feel and look of the ferns and bushes are quite refreshing as you cycle on your last stretch of the day. The grade is very slight here, and sometimes downhill through the Pass of Aberglaslyn. Mountains rise up in the distance, but here the water flows through rich meadows where the sheep seem content (one rebel strained through the fence to try for the greener grass). After 3 miles the road narrows and passes a splendid view of the river from a bridge. Keep going toward Beddgelert; the road rises seriously now past hills overflowing with rhododendrons. You'll come into **Beddgelert** within a mile.

Beddgelert is like a miniature version of Betws-y-Cœd. Everywhere you look from this little village you see the grandeur of the Snowdonia region, with the surrounding mountains ablaze with rhododendrons during the summer. William Wordsworth left this village for the famous dawn ascent of Mt. Snowdon, which became the subject matter for several of his poems. Part of the romantic flavor of this town comes from the little river that flows directly through its center.

WHERE TO STAY AND DINE IN BEDDGELERT

We will always treasure the memories of the hotel that we stayed in here because of its gorgeous setting and because of its eccentric guests. The Sygun Fawr Country House Hotel (Beddgelert, Gwynedd LL55 4NE; tel. [076686]258) is reached by turning right in the center of town at the Prince Llewelyn Hotel. Secluded in a seventeenth-century Welsh manor house ¼ mile down the road, the Sygun Fawr has out its windows some of the best mountain views that we saw on any of our tours of Wales. The food is excellent here too. The only drawback to the Sygun Fawr is the epic climb that last few hundred yards to reach it. Unless you have Olympic-size thighs, you will probably find yourself pushing your bike up that last little way. Our room had the most ingenious little Murphy-bed-like shower that folded down from the wall. (Modest)

Just up the same road, another excellent choice for lodging is the Bryn Edlwys Country House Hotel (Beddgelert, Gwynedd LL55 4NB; tel. [076686]210). It also has fine views of the village and the surrounding mountains. (Medium)

If you want to dine outside one of the hotels, you can find a tearoom and a small café in the center of town. The village's largest hotel, The Royal Goat (Beddgelert, Gwynedd LL55 4YE; tel. [076686]224 or 343) also has a dining room with an extensive menu. (Medium)

DAILY SUMMARY

WALES TOUR

Day Four: Betws-y-Cœd to Beddgelert

(33 miles; moderate, with a challenging stretch)

- Leave the village by the A5, going east out of town.
- Take the right fork on A5 and A470 toward Dolgellau.
- Go immediately right on A470 (sign: Dolgellau).
- In 6 miles you come into Dolwyddelan.
- You climb for 3 miles, then head downhill.

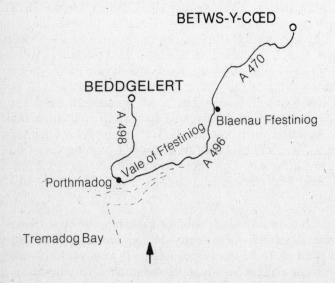

- Take the right fork on A496 and the next fork to Porthmadog after 1 mile.
- After 3 miles into the valley, turn toward Porthmadog.
- Stay on the A497 toward Porthmadog after passing through Penrhyndeudræth.
- Take a little side trip to the left to visit the Italianate village of Portmeirion. Return the same way and turn left at the T.
- After 2 miles you come into Porthmadog.
- Turn left here on A487 (sign: Cærnarfon).
- In Tremadog, take A487 right (sign: Beddgelert).
- Passing through Prenteg after 2 miles, keep following the signs to Beddgelert, which is 7½ miles from Porthmadog.

DAY FIVE: BEDDGELERT TO BEAUMARIS

(35 miles; moderate, challenging in morning)
Today we leave the mountain splendor of Snowdonia, going through its most famous pass and heading toward the seaside town of Cærnarfon, with its famous castle. You'll encounter three fairly challenging climbs in the morning; the rest of the 35-mile day is moderate.

The destination today is the picturesque fishing village of Beaumaris, which also has a thirteenth-century castle at the end of its main street. At the height of the season in August, you're likely to see as many boats in the harbor as the town has residents.

Leave the town on the A498 toward Capel Curig. You can drink in the splashes of pink on the hillsides from thousands of rhododendrons as you pedal along a pleasant winding road by the river, whose gentle roar pervades the air. The road is basically level in this first section. There are walking trails and several river vistas. After 1½ miles the river widens into the Llyn Dinas to your right, then the road begins to rise and fall over gentle hills. More forest appears, and you cross a bridge into what must be sheep heaven. Without question, this is the most beautiful place we've seen in all of Wales; it's truly breathtaking. A flock of white birds sailed across the deep green hills as the river and the Llyn Gynant widen on your left, 4 miles from Beddgelert. The air is an intoxicating, fresh combination of water, ferns, and trees. The road climbs a gentle hill past a stone barn with the valley opening into the distance. The climb continues moderately for 3 miles through spectacular views of the craggy mountains and river valley. The road is narrow at times, but the cars don't race along. There's a waterfall here that we saw from our hotel window.

Take a left on the A4086. You may first want to refuel at the Pen-y-Gwryd Hotel before tackling the pass. The grade starts up moderately, with a view over your left shoulder of the valley beyond the rock walls. After a mile you come to the Pey-y-Pass, where lots of tourists take the hiking path at the summit. The pass may look worse than it is, as it's downhill from here. You'll pass a jumble of rocks under the sheer cliffs off to the right and a combination of green and rock face on the crests to the left. The clouds can shroud the very tops of the mountains even when the valley is sunny. At times, many backpackers cluster at a point about 2 miles down the pass. A small waterfall joins the river flowing next to the stone wall. Trees begin to reappear after the austere higher land descends about 3 miles, and some B&Bs dot this imposing setting. Having come 4½ miles from the summit you go through **Llanberis,** where the road is level for ½ mile. It rises again moderately past a mining operation and the Llyn Padarn. About 2½ miles from Llanberis is the Snowdon Mountain Railway that you can take to the top of Mt. Snowdon; it costs the equivalent of approximately $15 per person. There are also shops and snacks available. A county park and several crafts shops line the road. Just out of town the road rises again in a moderate hill for a little over ½ mile. Twisting and opening over the river, the road becomes more level and passes cottages before the road widens, leaving the pass.

Continue on the A4086 toward Cærnarfon. This 4-mile stretch rolls uphill through more utilitarian homes, into **Llanrug,** a small town of limited appeal. Cresting a small hill you reenter green lands with the rounded trees and fields of sheep so characteristic of this area.

Continue to the right over the bridge toward Cærnarfon, and follow the signs to stay on A4086. The road narrows in places and passes a nursery and several B&Bs.

You enter **Cærnarfon** as the spacing of the houses gradually grows more dense. This is a large town on the Menai Strait.

Follow the signs to the Town Centre.

Follow the signs to (Castel) Castle. The busy town center forbids motor traffic, but you can walk your bicycle through. We recommend a lunch stop here as well as a visit to the castle, probably the best known of all Welsh castles. Another of Edward I's projects, this edifice took thirty-seven years to complete. Prince Charles received his investiture as Prince of Wales here in 1969. The castle is set at the mouth of the River Seiont and was built to secure the town (only partly successfully, as the Welsh swarmed over and killed the English here in 1294). The large castle has several towers, a moat, and houses a regimental museum; the structure dominates the town, which benefits from the many visitors who tour it each year.

One of the pleasures of visiting Cærnarfon is strolling around the streets listening to Welsh being spoken. In fact, we heard more Welsh than English being used here. As we stood in line at a supermarket waiting to buy our lunch supplies, we were charmed to hear the checkout girl switching effortlessly between Welsh and English, depending on whom she was talking to. The best bet down here is the excellent selection of bakeries, as well as tearooms, which also offer sandwiches, meat pasties, and soups. If you want to eat on the run, there's a large open-air market on the square also.

Leave town on the A487 toward Bangor. This road takes you back through town past the little shops of the main section.

At the roundabout after a few blocks take the A487 toward Bangor, to follow the Menai Strait. The houses you pass here are rather elegant, facing the straits with splendid views. High stone walls line the slightly uphill road under the shade of wonderful old trees. Meadows roll down the short distance to the water, and hills with grazing cattle rise to the right. After 3 miles the road brings you into the fine fishing village of **Port Dinorwic,** through the narrow lane off the main street with its neat row houses. Several picturesque stone cottages and a charming stone pub line the road just out of town.

At the roundabout take the left fork on the A487 toward Holyhead. The road turns moderately uphill here past a high stone wall for ¼ mile, then levels out.

At the next roundabout follow the sign toward Bangor (A487). Up a short, gentle hill through trees and meadows, you'll come to another roundabout.

Follow the sign to the left over the Menai Bridge. This narrow bridge has a bike and pedestrian path that allows you a great view of the straits.

Take the A545 toward Beaumaris at the next roundabout. You'll immediately ride through the center of **Portthæthwy,** where trucks ("lorries") have the habit of stopping in the middle of the street, creating severe jams. Little islands dot the channel as you ride gently uphill through rich, vine-covered walls enclosing fragrant trees. This largely residential area skirts the straits. You'll get peeks of the water through the breaks in the wall, then a more unimpeded view of the fishing boats and wooden piers with the green banks of the opposite shore. The road is winding and somewhat uphill through these 5 miles to **Beaumaris,** our destination for the evening.

WHERE TO STAY AND DINE IN BEAUMARIS

The best views in town are out the windows of the Bulkely Arms (Castle Street, Beaumaris, Isle of Anglesey LL58 8AW;

tel. STD [0248]810415). On a clear day you can see across the yacht harbor to the hills in the distance. The hotel has fully equipped rooms (many with sea views), and a superb restaurant which, even if you aren't staying here, is probably the best place in town to eat. The red carpets and bustling lounge just inside the entrance contribute to the hotel's warm, jovial atmosphere. (Medium)

A few miles outside of Beaumaris you'll find a small, but very fine guesthouse, the Ty'n Pistyll (Beach Road, Llanddona, Beaumaris, Gwynedd LL58 8UN; tel. [0248]811224). All their rooms have sea views and all the comforts of home, including hair driers and tea and coffee facilities. (Modest–Medium)

There are a tea and crepe shop on the main street and a couple of pleasant, airy restaurants in case you decide not to dine in your hotel.

WHAT TO SEE AND DO IN BEAUMARIS

The castle, also built by Edward I, is right in the heart of town. It is worth an hour or two, as is the Old Gael, which dates from 1829. If you happen to be here in June, there is an annual festival, with music, poetry, and theater. We found the main attractions here to be the long seawalks and the quiet back lanes of the environs.

DAILY SUMMARY

WALES TOUR

Day Five: Beddgelert to Beaumaris

(35 miles; moderate, challenging in morning)

- Leave Beddgelert on A498 toward Capel Curig.
- After a moderate 3-mile climb, turn left on A4086.
- After a mile you come to the Pey-y-Pass, where the road turns downhill.

- 4½ miles from the summit, you pass through Llanberis.
- Continue on A4086 (sign: Cærnarfon).
- 4 more miles lead into Llanrug.
- Continue to the right over a bridge toward Cærnarfon, staying on A4086.
- Follow the signs to Town Centre in Cærnarfon and to the castle.
- Leave town on A487 (sign: Bangor).
- After a few blocks, take A487 at the roundabout toward Bangor, which follows the Menai Strait.
- In 3 miles you pass through Port Dinorwic.
- Take the left fork on A487 at the roundabout (sign: Holyhead).
- At the next roundabout follow the sign toward Bangor on A487.
- After a short hill, follow the sign left over the Menai Bridge, taking the side pedestrian path.
- Turn toward Beaumaris on A545 at the next roundabout, which takes you immediately through Portthæthwy.
- In 5 miles you reach Beaumaris.

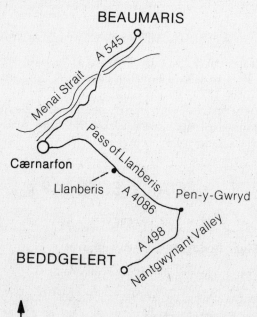

DAY SIX: THE ISLE OF ANGLESEY— BEAUMARIS TO HOLYHEAD

(47 miles; easy to moderate)
Our Wales tour culminates today with a winding 47-mile excursion across the wild back roads of the Isle of Anglesey. This longer day has easy to moderate terrain toward the destination of Holyhead. From Holyhead you can take a ferry to Ireland if you are heading that way.

Leave town on the B5109 toward Llanddona and Pentræth in the middle of the main street. This narrow part leads through charming row houses and uphill steeply under a stone bridge and into forest and field. The hill crests after a little less than a mile.

Stay on the road toward Pentræth. This country lane bends and curves through the familiar hedgerows surrounding the pastures and groves of this peaceful area. Your route is up and down moderate hills with little traffic.

After 3 miles, take the right fork toward Pentræth. Lounging cattle graced the low hills as we passed here last. The road continues up and down dale, never more than moderately and briefly, as you pedal past a farm B&B and the tree-covered hills to your right. Farms dot the terrain at regular intervals here; you turn through deeper woodlands for a short stretch.

After 3 miles you enter Pentræth, where you turn right on the B5109 toward Amlwch. A rather steep uphill takes the first ¼ mile on this road which then levels out through a residential area of white stone homes. Another slight uphill gives you a view of the Redwharf Bay and hills across the water. Stay on the road to Amlwch. Follow the slight uphill the rest of the 2 miles into **Benllech,** which has a popular beach and a charming downtown area.

Turn left on the B5108. (sign: Llangefni) A sharp, short uphill takes you inland past the outlying houses of Benllech past a rare horse pasture.

After almost 3 miles turn left on the B5110 toward Llangefni. Stay on the B5110 all the way to town. The winding, basically level road goes through pleasant countryside with a more arid feel than the deep greens of Snowdonia. Working farms appear frequently, as do fat sheep. A few rolling hills vary the ease of your ride after about 3 miles. The winds can whip across here, which probably explains the wealth of hedges and lines of trees. Watch for well-tended homes and stone cottages, some with leaded pane windows. You come into **Llangefni** 7 miles from Benllech.

At the T intersection just into town, turn right, then take a quick left on the A5114 (A5) toward Bangor. This section is a little over a mile. You ride on a wide road with long vistas of fields.

Turn left on A5 toward Bangor. We'll keep you on this busy thoroughfare as little as possible (stay on the wide shoulder). After about a mile you come into **Pentre Berw.**

You'll see the isle spreading out, with the bay off in the distance as you crest the hill after ½ mile. The road snakes through gentle and moderate small hills, past carefully tended stone cottages and gardens with fields rolling off beyond. A stone bridge takes you into a more moderate uphill after 2 miles. Bramble bushes and vine-covered trees lead you into a small village with a pretty church. Leveling out, you'll begin to glimpse the Maltræth Bay through hedge openings. About 4 miles from Pentre Berw you enter **Newborough.**

Turn right at the T intersection toward Aberffraw and Rhosneigr on the A4080. After a few residential blocks you wind downhill past pine forest and meadows of wildflowers. Marshlands and pasture line the couple of miles into the tiny village of **Maltræth.** A short uphill glides out of town and around through farmland.

Turn left on the A4080 toward Aberffraw. A pretty little church lies around the corner as the road winds down through closely clustered houses. The road is level or downhill through this sandy, heathery countryside, with swaying grass tufts and low dunes. The tidy village of **Aberffraw** lies 3 miles from Maltræth.

Turn into town for lunch at the fish and chips shop or the Prince Llewelyn Hotel. If you follow the signs around to the tourist information shop, you'll find a nice little café and craft shop in the little square.

Leave town on the A4080 toward Rhosneigr. Gentle undulations in the basically flat road carry you through grasslands and pastures with low ribbons of stone walls. The next villages become visible as you crest a small hill and ride past a sandy beach along the coastline. The heady smell of ocean air will invigorate you as you cycle over small hills on a road where wildflowers bloom in season. About 3 miles takes you into **Llanfælog.**

Turn right on the A4080 (A5). You're turning inland once again to stay on the back roads. This smaller route winds over small hills and through acres of pastureland and shrubs for 3 miles. On a clear day you'll see most of the isle.

At the junction, turn left on A5. We'll take you a short distance on the busier A5 before turning onto the last scenic loop of the tour. You'll cycle up and over modest to moderate hills on this ample road with a clearly marked shoulder. The fields become more lush as you come, after 5 miles, into **Valley.**

Turn left here on the B4545. (sign: Tre-Arddur) Your level road angles through lightly colored houses with pretty sprawling gardens and bushes. The area has a resort feel, and the light is soft. Approximately 3 miles takes you into **Tre-Arddur Bay,** a comfortable-looking town with beach access if you're so inclined. A rare hill takes you up through the cream-colored houses behind the gray stone walls, then rolling over several small hills past some stone outcroppings and older homes into more heavily populated areas. There's just a ½ mile distance between Tre-Arddur Bay and **Holyhead.** As you come closer to the town center you may see large ships anchored in the harbor. Follow the road around the edge of the island past the beautiful green commons (excellent for picnicking) and the beautiful yacht harbor to get a sense of the scope of the town.

WHERE TO STAY AND DINE IN HOLYHEAD

Welcome to Holyhead, the end of the Wales tour. The best place to stay is not actually in Holyhead proper but in Tre-Arddur Bay 2½ miles down the road. There you will find the Tre-Arddur Bay Hotel (Tre-Arddur Bay, nr. Holyhead, Isle of Anglesey, Gwynedd LL65 2UN; tel. [0407]86301). This hotel has an indoor heated swimming pool, which you may appreciate if you have had to brave the Welsh elements to get here, as we did. All bedrooms come with private bath, color TV, and telephone. (Medium)

The tourist information center here handles all B&B bookings for this area as a free service. You can visit them just off the main street of town, or contact them in advance at: Wales Tourist Office, Salt Island Approach, Holyhead, Isle of Anglesey, Gwynedd LL65 1DR; tel. [0407]762622.

There are two good restaurants in Holyhead that serve the best of the region's seafood cuisine. These are the Zodiac Wine Bar, located on the main promenade with views of the harbor (tel. 4242), and the Lobster Pot (tel. 730241), outside of town on the A5025 up toward Carmel Head. (At the latter you can pick out your lobster from the tanks in the garden.) In town are many informal establishments including a Chinese takeaway and some fish and chips shops.

WHAT TO SEE AND DO IN HOLYHEAD

There are some interesting side trips you can make from Holyhead. For example, there is a road that you can take around Holyhead Mountain to Southstack Lighthouse. You'll see a sign off the promenade directing you. The little village of Rhoscolyn lies below Tre-Arddur Bay. It's at the southernmost tip of Holy Island. There is a good swimming beach in this picturesque village and some scenic walks from here along the cliffs. One in particular, a remarkable cliff formation called Bwa Du (Black Arch) will have you reaching for your camera. If you follow the signs to Southstack, you can visit Ellin's Tower Seabird Centre. Here you may get your first glimpse of the famous puffin, indigenous to this area.

DAILY SUMMARY

WALES TOUR

Day Six: The Isle of Anglesey—Beaumaris to Holyhead

(47 miles; easy to moderate)

- Leave Beaumaris on B5109 in the middle of the main street (signs: Llanddona, Pentræth).
- Stay on the road toward Pentræth.
- After 3 miles, turn on the right fork toward Pentræth, which you'll enter in another 3 miles.
- Turn right on B5109 toward Amlwch.
- Stay on the road toward Amlwch, which takes you into Benllech in 2 miles.
- Take a left on B5108 (sign: Llangefni).
- In almost 3 miles, turn left on B5110 toward Llangefni and stay on B5110 all the way into town, 7 miles from Benllech.
- At the T intersection just into town, turn right, then take an immediate left on A5114 (A5) toward Bangor.
- After a little over a mile, take a left on A5 toward Bangor.
- In about 1 mile, you come into Pentre Berw, and in another 4, Newborough.
- Turn right on A4080 at the T intersection (sign: Aberffraw, Rhosneigr).
- In a couple of miles, after passing through Maltræth uphill, turn left on A4080 toward Aberffraw.

- Abberffraw is about 3 miles from Maltræth.
- Leave Abberffraw on A4080 toward Rhosneigr.
- After 3 miles, in Llanfælog, turn right on A4080 (A5).
- In 3 more miles, take a left on A5.
- You'll pass through Valley in 5 miles.
- Turn left here on B4545 (sign: Tre-Arddur).
- 3 miles bring you through Tre-Arddur, and 2½ more into Holyhead.

GETTING BACK TO LONDON

One of the reasons we have ended the tour in Holyhead is because it is convenient and easy to get back to London from here, as well as to any other point in England reachable by rail. Direct trains are available, arriving back at London's Euston Station after approximately a five-hour ride.

THE HIGHLANDS AND

ISLANDS OF

SCOTLAND

MANY PEOPLE THINK OF SCOTLAND AS THE MOST MAGNIF-
icent country on earth, and for good reason. The scenery is
splendid, and the people, despite their reputation for stingi-
ness, are more than generous with their hospitality. These
hardy, frugal people are often quiet and shy; their friendli-
ness, however, is undisputed. As far as terrain goes, there is
something here for everyone: moor, mountain, stream, and
meadow. We have chosen a route that takes you, in our opinion, through the best of the best.

Scottish money is different from the English, though
worth the same and interchangeable with the British pound.
The language is not as interchangeable, at least to these North
American ears. Nowhere in the British Isles do we say
"Hunh?" and "Could you repeat that?" more than in the
highlands.

Geologically, Scotland is the oldest part of the British
Isles. Humans have been up there for a long time, too: Evidence puts mankind in Scotland since the most recent Ice

Age. There are many prehistoric monuments, some of which
you'll pass on our tour, that are reminders of the ancient days.
The Scots have been fiercely independent for as long as anyone can remember. Even the Romans couldn't tame the former residents, a short dark people called the Picts, and had
to retreat down south behind Hadrian's Wall. Nowadays Scotland is peopled more by the fair-skinned, red-bearded blood-
line, but you will still see the distant offspring of the Picts in
the rural countryside.

Today the entire population of Scotland is not much over
five million, and most of those live in the lowlands. The part
you'll be riding through is not very densely populated. And
if you really want to get away from it all, Scotland has a
couple of hundred islands sprinkled off its coasts. Some of
these don't even have sheep on them (in Scotland you are
never more than 40 miles from salt water, and it seems as if
you're hardly ever more than a mile or so from a sheep).

GETTING TO THE HIGHLANDS

We have always taken the train up from the south and started
our tours from Inverness (except for one occasion when we
went over to the Ft. William area to begin). The tour we
describe here begins at Inverness. By train, the journey will
take you the better part of a day. Most of the trains to Scotland leave from London's Euston Station. Sometimes you can
get a train straight through to Inverness, but on other routes
you may have to change trains at Edinburgh. A couple of
times we have taken the bullet train to Edinburgh, then
switched to the slower one on to Inverness. On two occasions
we took a sleeper, which is fun even though we tend not to
sleep very much on them. If you want to fly in, you can
use the airport at Inverness. There are frequent shuttles from
Heathrow to Edinburgh, then you can transfer to a smaller
plane to Inverness. Short air hops in Europe are surprisingly
expensive, so if you are on any kind of budget you may want
to take the train. We love trains anyway, so we have never
even thought of flying into Scotland.

TOURING THE HIGHLANDS: AN INTRODUCTION

After our three tours of Scotland, we have devised a plan which will allow you to see and experience as much as you can of the highlands in the shortest time and with the least mileage. Scotland is a place that one could spend months or probably a lifetime touring by bicycle. Recognizing, however, that most of our readers will not have unlimited time, we've done our best to devise a tour of approximately a week that would afford a rich taste of this wonderful region.

We've found it best to begin the tour in the capital city of the highlands, Inverness, and to spend the first two days there making day loops to the scenic territory around the city. One reason for staying in Inverness for the first few days of the tour is that it would be a really fine city to explore even if it weren't the gateway to highlands touring.

INVERNESS

Inverness is one of the most beautiful and friendly cities we've ever visited. Shakespeare's famous King Duncan had a castle here by the eleventh century, and even earlier St. Columba was supposed to have paid a visit to the King of the Picts somewhere in this vicinity. The downside of the strategic importance of Inverness is that it's been at the center of many battles over the years, with the nearby battlefield of Culloden being the most important. Its popularity as a place to hold battles results in a dearth of ancient buildings in and around the town; they all got sacked a long time ago. Most of the buildings in town date from the nineteenth century, when the arrival of the railroad brought a fresh wave of prosperity to the town. The completion, in 1822, of the Caledonian Canal (which flows through the center of town) was another factor in the town's evolution into current status.

There are many worthwhile things to see and do in Inverness. If you go in September, you can attend the bagpipe competitions which have been held since 1781. If you are like the authors—for whom a little bit of bagpiping goes a long way—you may want to explore other options in September. There is a particularly fine museum and art gallery near the center of town with an exhibit on the first floor called "Inverness: Hub of the Highlands." It's a good way to get oriented to the potentials of this region. The cathedral here is worth a visit to see the pulpit of carved stone and other elaborate decorations.

The city is built on either side of the Ness River, the banks of which are lined with stately homes, some of which are now guest houses. The banks of the river make a fine place for an evening stroll or ride. In this northern land the summer light does not end until nearly 11 P.M. Since we first visited here in the late '70s, we have seen many changes in the city. Most recently the downtown area has undergone a major face-lift. One of the main streets was developed into a pedestrian mall with a large Marks and Spencer and several American imports, such as a tasteful McDonald's. Shopping malls are also springing up around town in the new system of one-way streets and large car parks. This development, although increasing the city's resemblance to shopping malls all over the world, has decreased the congestion and diesel fumes while increasing possibilities for shopping and exploring.

WHERE TO STAY AND DINE IN INVERNESS

There are two broad categories of lodging in Inverness. Bed and breakfast and guesthouses are at the lower end of the budget spectrum. B&Bs are a very good bargain in this town.

On our most recent visit we stayed at one of the best appointed B&Bs we have ever visited for the bargain basement price of £10 per person (or about $35 for both of us). This little treasure was at 9 Sunnybank Avenue, Inverness IV2 4HD (tel. [0463]233835). (Modest)

On another evening we slept at the Aberfeldy Lodge (11 Southside Road, Inverness, IV2 3BG; tel. [0463]231120). Our comfortable, large *en suite* room there, with bed and breakfast was also quite reasonable. (Medium)

On the higher end of the budget spectrum you will find the hotels of Inverness, even the more modest of which tend to be quite pricey. Two comfortable ones are the Dunain Park Hotel, on six acres of woodland and serving a French-inspired cuisine (Inverness IV3 6JN; tel. [0463]230512) and the Glen Mhor Hotel, located on the river in the downtown area (9–12 Ness Bank, Inverness IV2 4SC; tel. [0463]234308). (both Top)

We want to make special mention of the tourist information bureau in downtown Inverness because of the heroic job they do coping with the large numbers of people who visit them each day. We have always found them to be patient and friendly. They book beds at hundreds of accommodations in the area for a very modest fee (which is deducted from the cost of your lodgings). They also offer a "book a bed ahead" service, which allows you to make reservations for out-of-town locations.

One place we always go back to when we're in Inverness is Dickens International Restaurant (77 Church Street; tel. [0463]22450). It has a wide range of interesting ethnic tastes, including Mauritanian curries, which we have never seen anywhere else. You can get traditional dishes here as well as Chinese and Indonesian innovations. (Medium)

Being devotees of Indian food, we sought out as many Indian restaurants as we could in Inverness. One of the best was Rose of Bengal (4–6 Ness Walk, Inverness; tel. [0463]233831). Their tandoori king prawns turned out to be one of the most memorable feasts on our most recent tour of Scotland. The staff was most hospitable and efficient. (Medium)

In the downtown area there are two relatively new establishments that are good and quite popular. Haydens Café Bar (37 Queensgate; tel. [0463]236969) has light food, espresso, and a huge selection of beer and wines. (Modest)

If you're hungering for something North American, visit the Pancake Place (25/27 Church Street, tel. [0463]226156), which has burgers and other fare in addition to pancakes. (Modest)

WHAT TO SEE AND DO AROUND INVERNESS.

Just strolling around Inverness is always fun because of the colorful characters you meet in the most ordinary interactions.

The castle, built in the nineteenth century on the site of many previous castles, is now used for city offices. The Town House is a Gothic building worth poking your head in to see the crystal chandeliers and the portrait of Bonnie Prince Charlie. Inverness has a huge swimming pool, complete with sauna, jacuzzi, and an exercise room. You can rent towels and swimming suits there if you forgot yours. Visitors are welcome at all of the four local bowling greens. These are open late into the evening, and are a great place to meet locals. Scotland's busiest theater, the Eden Court (tel. [0463]221718), which hosts everything from plays to rock to opera, is near downtown. It seats eight hundred people and has a movie theater and restaurant as part of its complex.

For a change of pace, the Ness Islands, near Inverness, can be reached via bridges, and offer very secluded ambling opportunities if you tire of big city bustle.

DAY ONE: CASTLE AND CAIRN LOOP

(26 miles, easy to moderate)
Inverness is a big city, and all the exits are busy. We will take the least busy. Today's 26-mile loop through the countryside and to historic monuments covers easy and moderate terrain.

Leave right by the railroad station on the B865 toward Wick and Perth. This is a four-lane road for a mile or so, but there is a wide sidewalk on which to ride. This section of town has outlying hotels and some industry.

At the roundabout, about I mile out of town, take the B9006 toward Culloden Moor. An easy upward slope takes you into flowery meadows and green trees.

Stay on the main road to the left to remain on the B9006, which you will take all the way to Croy. Exercise caution along here, because the traditional Scottish reserve melts the moment they get behind the wheel. They become wild, daring drivers.

Just under 2 miles from your start, continue on the B9006 at the large roundabout. The road has some hills here as it continues through the "suburbs." Stay on the B9006. Some level plateaus extend for a few hundred feet, but then you head gently upward again. As you crest the hill you get your first look at the Moray Firth over the pastures and pines and bright yellow gorse and broom bushes (in the spring and summer) that roll down to it. Culloden Battlefield is 6 miles outside Inverness to your right. Make a turn to view the most famous battlefield of the area. If you have even a drop of Scottish blood in your heritage, Culloden is a must-see. This windy, bleak moor was the scene of the terrible battle in 1746 when Bonnie Prince Charlie was defeated by the government troops loyal to King George II. The battlefield is open and free to the public, with a series of markers which explain the location of the troops and other facts of the battle. This was the last battle fought on British soil.

Continue on the B9006 to your right after leaving Culloden. (sign: Cawdor Castle) Our morning trip takes us into Nairn. We'll visit Cawdor and the Cairns of Clava in the afternoon. Gorse and broom punctuate the countryside here on this basically level road. About 2 miles from the battlefield the road rises on a slight incline through a small forest and rides the ridge with green forested hills visible to the right across the valley. Cattle graze in fields enclosed by a low stone wall. The firth and **Croy** appear 4 miles after Culloden.

Take the right fork on B9091 just on entering town. You'll pass several attractive cottages before heading into deeper forest on this generally flat pavement.

After 1½ miles you come to an X intersection; take the road straight across toward Nairn. This pleasant countryside is thick with gorse, broom, grasses, and forest. The even path opens into a long view of hills and pastureland, with solid stone farmhouses at intervals. Follow the signs to Nairn. After 3½ miles, you'll encounter your first hill, which elevates you to views of the far forest and firth. The road turns and rolls a little over slight hills and restful farmlands, and 5 miles from Croy you'll enter **Nairn,** that most optimistic of places, a Scottish seaside resort. Although we have not personally witnessed the sun shining on any of our trips through here, on several occasions we were told, "You should have been here last week." (This particular phrase is heard quite often as one tours the British Isles.) Nairn is basically a pleasant town worth a lunch stop and stroll around. Speaking of lunch, there is a very popular small café called the Tea Cosy right on High Street. It has floral tablecloths on the small tables, and wonderful pastries. You can also get sandwiches, baked and stuffed potatoes, and homemade soups. If you're in the mood for a meat pie, there is also a large butcher shop nearby. A café and a fish and chips shop are located just on coming into the town center. Poppies Tea Room, a pleasant place for light fare, nestles on High Street in the town center. The beach and views of the firth, are just down the street.

Leave town up High Street on the B9090 toward Cawdor.

Follow the signs to Cawdor on B9090. This smooth and level road quickly takes you into open countryside with clusters of trees and large fields. You'll turn and enter a very pretty forested area after 2 miles. Forestland is something of a rarity in Scotland, which on the whole was deforested a thousand years ago. Canopies of trees overhang the road and you'll see the castle apparently nestled among them after 5 miles.

Turn right at the signs for Cawdor Castle. The castle of Cawdor, despite its historical legends, looks surprisingly modern compared to some of the truly medieval castles to be seen farther south. Although we are not serious castle buffs, we very much enjoyed touring this one; the duck pond and the lush natural setting make it a pleasant stop even without a trip inside. If you do go inside, be sure to see the tapestry bedroom and the seventeenth-century four-poster bed. Shakespeare immortalized the name of Cawdor, for it was promised to Macbeth by the witches. Supposedly, Duncan was murdered here. In reality, the thanes of Cawdor built the castle in the fourteenth century and made it the seat of the family throne.

Leave Cawdor Castle on the road to the left to rejoin the B9090.

Turn left at the T intersection after a block toward Inverness. The village of Cawdor and the small church are quite beautiful. The open fields here rise up to lines of forest on this easy, winding road through farms and fields of sheep.

After about a mile, take the left (straight) fork toward Dalroy and Craggie. This narrow, stone wall–lined road winds through fern-covered hills and up a gentle slope into forest; grass tufts cap the old stone. Bundles of gorse and broom dot the landscape, and charming farms and cottages line the road. The occasional vivid lupine pops up, and you pedal with a view across the valley to the site of the morning's ride. After 2 miles you'll ascend a moderate hill past homes and gardens, cresting after ½ mile over the valley. The countryside has wide open fields here as the road weaves over gentle hills through a large patch of gorse and into a small forest.

A great view of the arched, red stone viaduct appears before you head over a stream and through a section lined with the spikes and flowers of gorse. You're cycling through slight rolling hills here.

6½ miles after your fork, turn right at the small sign to Clava. You'll wind through a farm and downhill into the valley past a country B&B, then up a short hill and around neatly tended fields and pasture. A moderate downhill drops into the valley floor, which passes the Clava Cairns on your left.

Do stop to walk through these remarkable burial mounds with their accompanying standing stones. The magical, mystical feel of the site is palpable even now, four thousand years after it was first built. The magnificent old trees of the glen add to its hushed aura. There are three cairns, or burial mounds, each surrounded by a circle of standing stones. The cairns themselves are encircled by a mound of small boulders, graded from largest at the base to smaller and more rounded near the top. Not much is known about this site from a scientific perspective. It seems very likely, though, that since the highest standing stones and the openings of some of the cairns are toward the southwest, there was some connection between the winter solstice and death in the religious beliefs of these early inhabitants.

Leave the cairns to your left with the viaduct visible in the distance.

Turn left at the (unmarked) T corner. Passing over a pretty stream, you'll ride up a moderate hill for almost ½ mile past a lovely farm B&B.

At the X intersection a mile from the cairns go straight across toward Culloden Battlefield.

Turn left after 100 yards or so toward Culloden Battlefield. You'll pass this site returning toward Inverness. You'll have an excellent view of the Moray Firth and Inverness riding this direction, and your earlier mild uphill becomes a pleasant downhill.

Continue on the B9006. You'll cross the A9.
At the large roundabout take the route toward Town Centre on the B865.

Signs to Town Centre and "long stay" under the overpass take you the remaining mile or so back into **Inverness.**

DAILY SUMMARY

SCOTLAND TOUR

Day One: Castle and Cairn Loop

(26 miles; easy to moderate)

- Leave Inverness right by the railroad station on B865 (signs: Wick, Perth).
- At the roundabout after about a mile, take B9006 toward Culloden Moor.
- You will remain on B9006 all the way into Croy, at the roundabout after 2 miles and after Culloden Battlefield (sign: Cawdor Castle).
- You'll reach Croy 4 miles after Culloden.
- Turn right at the fork here on B9091 at the town entrance.
- Continue following the signs 5 miles into Nairn.
- Leave Nairn up High Street on B9090 toward Cawdor.
- Follow the signs to Cawdor on B9090.
- Cawdor Castle is visible in 5 miles.
- Turn right at the signs for Cawdor Castle.
- Leave the castle on the road to the left to rejoin the B9090.
- Turn left at the T intersection after a block (sign: Inverness).
- After a mile, take the left (straight) fork toward Dalroy and Craggie.
- In 6½ miles from the last fork, turn right at the small sign to Clava and the Clava Cairns.
- Leave the cairns to your left.
- Turn left at the (unmarked) T corner.
- At the X intersection a mile from the cairns go straight across toward Culloden Battlefield.

- Turn left after 100 yards or so toward Culloden Battlefield.
- Continue on B9006 back into Inverness.
- After crossing the A9, take the route toward Town Centre on B865 at the roundabout.

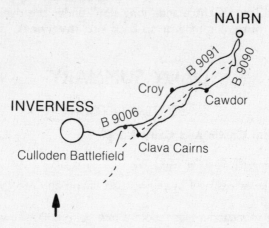

DAY TWO: BLACK ISLE LOOP

(56 miles; primarily easy)
The Black Island is neither black nor an island. Rather, it's a green peninsula. It is surprising to find such a haven of unspoiled beauty between the bustle of Inverness and the industrialized north shore of Cromarty Firth. The Black Isle is surrounded on three sides by three Firths, the Beauly, Moray, and Cromarty. Down the central highland of the Isle runs a ridge of forest. Much of the rest of the Isle is rural farmland. This is a longer, 50-mile day, as many of the subsequent days will be. The terrain, however, is primarily easy.

Leave Inverness on the A9 over the large Kessock bridge for today's tour. There is a sidewalk across the whole bridge that we suggest you take. After the bridge the road is busy with fast cars. The road is wide, though, with a marked shoulder.

Turn right on the B9161 toward Munlochy after almost 2 miles. We carefully studied the alternatives to this section of busy road and concluded that in the interests of mileage, a short jaunt with traffic was a necessary choice. This fairly level road looks out over hilly farmland and a manor house in the midst of a grove of trees. You'll come into trees yourself after less than a mile, after which the road bends downhill and through very green, rich fields. A short uphill brings you into **Munlochy** after about 2 miles. You'll continue uphill to the intersection.

Turn right on the A832 toward Cromarty. The Munlochy Bay reflects the surrounding forestland to your right. The road inclines on a slight uphill for about a mile, with wildflowers, stone walls, and fields into the far distance. Many shades of green cap the treetops to your left as you ride through **Avoch,** about 2 miles from Munlochy. Avoch is an attractive village on the water, with small boats in the harbor. You'll skirt the water here, separated by a stone wall and rock pilings. Another 1½ miles brings you into **Fortrose,** another very pretty town, with lovely stone buildings and sailboats bobbing on the bay. This town is the commercial center of the Black Isle. Here you'll find an old cathedral set in a quiet backdrop of lawn. To find the cathedral, look for the sign on the main street directing you off to the right. We suggest a stop for morning coffee or tea and a snack here, as lunch will not be for another 20 miles or so. Out of town you reenter glorious greenery again and immediately come through **Rosemarkie,** with narrow streets of red stone houses and Tudor-style cottages. The road just out of Rosemarkie rises moderately into deep forest on a beautiful section of road. The uphill, becoming easier, lasts for a mile and levels out briefly as you come to an intersection.

Turn left toward Balblair on the B9160. Another slight upgrade takes you under roadside trees with wide fields and gorse as company. This section of road has long, slow hills in it over a gentle incline. Lots of gorse, broom, and pines line the road. You'll crest the hills after 2 miles and see the Ben Wyvis mountains in the distance. The downhill continues into beautiful views of the Cromarty Bay.

Follow the road to the right toward Conon Bridge. An uphill through fields winds along the ridge with the bay on your right. About 5½ miles from Rosemarkie you come into **Balblair,** which you skirt by staying on the main road and *not* going toward Newhall Point. Last time we passed this way on a day in the middle of June, snow was still visible on the top of the far-off mountains. The road here is mostly flat and fairly straight in sections, with the Cromarty Firth, a beautiful length of gray-blue water ringed by towns and forest, on your right.

You'll see the road stretching along a straight ribbon into the distance, curling over short hills; there will be several opportunities to turn down to firthside to admire the view more closely. As you ride up this long but not steep hill you may notice how "northern" the terrain looks, especially across the firth, with forests of fir and barren mountains off in the distance. The long uphill crests after 3 miles.

Almost 12 miles from Balblair, turn right on the A862. This glorious downhill curves through the rural land with views of the water. You'll move along the curve of the bay with the bridge on the right.

Turn right on the A9 toward Wick for about 50 feet, then left on the B9163 toward the village of Conon Bridge. This somewhat rough but level road follows the water for ½ mile, then turns up a short hill past small farms and a large waterside estate.

Follow the signs to Conon Bridge. Cattle and sheep share the fields leading to the Firth and the hills on the opposite shore.

The hills of the Black Isle to your left are gentler and full of cattle.

Turn right after 4 miles at the T intersection on the A835, then a quick left to continue on the B9163. Just ¼ mile brings you into **Conon Bridge.**

At the junction with A862, turn right into town. There's a pub, the Drouthy Duck, advertising delicious food right across from the Conon Hotel, which offers afternoon teas and bar meals.

Leave Conon Bridge on the A862 toward Beauly. The contrast of terrain visible in this area is one of Scotland's main attractions. Lovely homes and estates abound here.

After 3½ miles on this road, follow the A862 over the bridge and to the right. (sign: Inverness) You'll ride through lovely fields and pastureland with the Ben Wyvis mountains still visible for a time. This section of road has particularly lovely homes and estates. **Muir of Ord,** into which you pass over a bridge, has many charming red stone houses. You'll continue to follow the signs toward Inverness and the A862 all the way around the Firth of Beauly. The road is mainly level and fairly smooth, with several slight rises around bends. You pass through **Beauly,** a small, very pretty village, 4½ miles from Muir of Ord. You'll turn over the Beauly River out of town and enter a section of more forest and hilly pastures before having, after about 5 miles, an unimpeded view of the Beauly Firth. You're right on the water here just before coming into Inverness, with the Kessock Bridge looming ahead.

At the roundabout, follow the signs to Town Centre over the bridge back into **Inverness.**

DAILY SUMMARY

SCOTLAND TOUR

Day Two: Black Isle Loop

(56 miles; primarily easy)

- Exit Inverness on A9 over the large Kessock bridge.
- Turn right on B9161 toward Munlochy after almost 2 miles.
- In Munlochy, after about 2 miles, take a right on A832 (sign: Cromarty).
- You'll pass through Avoch 2 miles from Munlochy, and Fortrose after another 1½ miles. Rosemarkie appears very shortly.
- A mile out of Rosemarkie, turn left on B9160 (sign: Balblair).
- Follow the road toward the right after 2 + miles (sign: Conon Bridge).
- In Balblair, 5½ miles from Rosemarkie, continue on the main road.
- Almost 12 miles from Balblair, turn right on A862.
- After the downhill, take a right on A9 toward Wick for only 50

feet or so, then left on B9163 toward the village of Conon Bridge.
- Follow the signs to Conon Bridge.
- After 4 miles on A835 go right at the T intersection, then take a quick left to stay on B9163 the ¼ mile into Conon Bridge.
- At the junction with A862, turn right into town.
- Leave Conon Bridge on A862 toward Beauly.
- After 3½ miles follow the A862 over the bridge and to the right (sign: Inverness).
- You'll follow the A862 all around the Firth of Beauly. Muir of Ord is visible after a few miles, Beauly in another 4½ miles. Another 12 miles or so brings you back into Inverness.

DAY THREE: INVERNESS TO INVERMORISTON

(50 miles; easy to moderate)
Once, some years ago, we chose to take the train to Kyle of Lochalsh rather than cycling the two days' journey. We rented bikes to go around the Isle, and all we could round up were three-speed clunkers. Nowadays, in the era of the mountain bike, better options are available, although we still do not recommend relying on rental bikes except in certain circumstances. Here is one occasion when a rental might be fun. We did it by taking the gorgeous train ride to Kyle of Lochalsh, cycling around the island, then taking the train back to Inverness. You might want to spend longer than this, because the Isle of Skye can be a lovely place to ride. If you want to rent a bike on the Isle of Skye, contact the Cycle Shop at Kyleakin, where the ferry drops you off (tel. [0599]4816). They have over one hundred bikes for rent. A fully equipped mountain bike currently will run you the equivalent of $20 a day. Another option, of course, would be to bring your own bike on the train to Kyle of Lochalsh.

We suggest cycling to the Isle of Skye and returning on the train. Do check the return train schedules to Inverness when you plan your last day's exploratory side trips.

If you have time left over on your return, a possible side trip would be down the A851 to explore the Sleat Peninsula. Sometimes called the "garden of Skye" because of its rich array of foliage and vegetation, Sleat can offer a refreshing alternative, especially if the weather is bleak. The Sleat Peninsula also has a couple of castles, Knock Castle and Dunsgiath Castle, both former strongholds of the MacDonald clan.

Your third day's 50 miles takes you through the remarkable countryside and back roads of the lesser-known lochs clustered around Loch Ness. You'll end the day on the western side of Loch Ness, a jumping-off point to the western highlands.

Leave Inverness from in front of the tourist information office by heading down Church Street to the lights. Turn left here and follow the road around to the stoplight intersection.

Go straight across on the B862 toward Holm.

Stay on the main road, *not* along the river. You'll exit through one of the prettiest parts of Inverness, with the Ness River to your right and tree-shaded houses to your left.

Turn left at the sign to Essich after 1½ miles. The road bends and turns uphill moderately for under ¼ mile. You're continuing to pedal through the lovely outlying homes of Inverness, which seems to specialize in well-maintained stone houses.

At the roundabout almost 3 miles from town, take the route straight across toward Essich. The route turns more rural here, and the narrower road winds on a moderate upgrade, with the valley beyond the green fields to your right. You continue a gentle uphill to **Essich,** 4 miles from Inverness, and uphill past this tiny village, through pastures with horses and sheep, gorse and grass, for a little over 1½ miles on a great backroad bicycling route. You're on the crest of a ridge here with hills to both sides. Some 2 miles from Essich, you come into views of the lochs which are scattered throughout this region, of which Loch Ness is the most famous. Loch Ashie, on your left, is a small lake surrounded by pines and grass. The last time we took this route we had it virtually to ourselves.

At the intersection about 4 miles from Essich take the left fork toward Loch Duntelchaig. This little road goes past Loch Ashie and open fields on gentle hills. Loch Duntelchaig opens to your right, reflecting the hills that surround three sides of this exquisite lake. A lovely little glen skirts the lake here, and you're often only feet from the smooth water's edge on this level section of pavement; across the water, cliffs come right down to the water's edge. Then you enter forest again and head up over gentle hills into heathery country, still skirting the lake. The moss-covered rocks and shades of red, gold, and gray against the green trees and gray-blue water are enchanting. The narrow path is quite twisty but basically level. After 3½ miles you come through **Dunlichy,** where you stay on the main road, such as it is. Glen and field alternate, as do up- and downhill on what is still basically level land. A gentle uphill winds through idyllic pastureland and past farms.

After another 2½ miles, turn right on the B851.

Just after turning you come into Invernarnie, turn right toward Orrogie. A lovely old stone church stands in **Farr,** a small village with winding stream and rich fields between the forests. You'll pass a pleasant tearoom and craft shop before you ride under a canopy of large trees on a slight uphill grade. Rhododendrons and forest mix here among homes kept with obvious pride. The road winds through genuine highlands country here, moors and crags spilling into forest and stream. The sweeping vistas extend for miles over contrasts between stark rock and rich fields. We had a fine coffee and flaky shortbread break for the modest sum of £2 at the Grouse & Trout Hotel, about 3 miles from Farr on the B851. The hotel is well-staffed by friendly people; we recommend your morning break here, or lunch, as their menu is varied, and the view is excellent. If the weather is good, outdoor tables are available.

Continue south on the B851 on into **Croachy,** another

tiny village set between mountain ridges in this long, lush valley. You'll find the road even here, by and large, winding through the valley. Outside the village 3 miles, you'll encounter a few more mild hills that begin to elevate your ride through the far end of the valley.

Stay on the road toward Errogie. The road winds on a steady, gentle to moderate incline, now into treeless moors of heather and the occasional cluster of bushes. Trees gather on the surrounding hills. Today you'll get a taste of just about everything Scotland has to offer. Lochs, craggy mountains, pine forests, moors, and fertile valleys are all visible at one spot here, about 5 miles out of Croachy.

Join the B862 and continue heading south. Another 1⅓ miles brings you into **Errogie,** on the shores of Loch Mhor.

Turn left on the B862 toward Gorthleck. The road goes through mild hills and dales beside the loch, a long narrow lake with many fingers. It's surrounded primarily by moors. You'll ride through tiny **Gorthleck** after 1½ miles, continuing beside the loch, which extends for many miles. Lots of gorse and broom decorate the roadside here on the slight upward slope of pavement. This single track road is ideal for bicycling, and we think you'll really enjoy the rich variety of scenery and the lack of tourist bustle. After about 3 miles the road briefly becomes a marked two-lane and continues to wind up and down slight hills through more trees and past a rocky stream. In the small village of **Whitebridge,** the road moves through a mountainous-feeling area where the air turns fragrant with pine. The wider route moves at first gently, then moderately uphill through the pass for about 3 miles, with the Monadhliath Mountains rising starkly to your left. At the crest you'll be able to stop and see Loch Ness in the valley to the right. You start the downhill roll here past these softer and denuded peaks that give the mountains here a friendly look. You descend to the shores of Loch Tarff, a small lake right next to Loch Ness but separated by a row of hills. As you leave the loch the road turns more steeply downhill by tree-studded hills, then more gently curving and rolling uphill for a little over ¼ mile. You'll see Loch Ness to your right. There are several opportunities to stop and view this large and famous lake as your route bends around the south end of the lake and into **Fort Augustus,** a former military settlement about 5 miles from the summit and full of red stone houses and tourist facilities. The watch for Nessie, the Loch Ness monster, is a big attraction around here, and it's not uncommon to hear people saying, "Yes, the weather was too warm [or too cold] for Nessie today; she didn't show." Nessie is always referred to as female.

You'll cycle beside Loch Ness for several miles now, sometimes just a few feet away, sometimes separated by a hedge of trees. The road is more established here, busier, and lined with vivid green trees and ferns. Almost 6 miles from Fort Augustus you'll enter **Invermoriston,** your stop for the night.

WHERE TO STAY AND DINE IN INVERMORISTON

At the junction with the A887, the Tudor-style Glenmoriston Hotel (Glenmoriston, IV3 6YA; tel. [0320]51206) has established a fine reputation in this highlands area. It has large, comfortable rooms, a well-equipped dining room, and tables for eating outdoors. (Medium)

On the A887 ½ mile out of town is the Weeford B&B (Invermoriston, Inverness-shire, IV3 6YA; tel. [0320]51291), with a beautiful view of the mountains. This nicely appointed home is run by John and Mavis House. (Modest)

Call ahead in general in this area, as things tend to book up fairly quickly.

If you have time here, you can make a 26-mile round trip up to Urquhart Castle (pronounced Urkit), on the shores of Loch Ness on the A82. Dramatically placed on a promontory overlooking the loch, the castle ruins have a history as rocky as their setting. The ride up is on a smooth but heavily trafficked road. You'll find that most of the terrain between Invermoriston and the castle is rocky, the route gently but steadily uphill. As you walk toward the castle you'll probably hear bagpipe music from one of the decorative bagpipers who stroll the grounds. Last time we were here we had a pleasant chat with one of them. He told us he'd had a brief sighting of Nessie four years before. Nearby, in the easy to get to but hard to pronounce village of Drumnadrochit, is the Loch Ness Monster exhibition. There are many photographs, along with displays showing the new technological attempts to find the creature. The loch is so deep (over 750 feet) that just about anything could be hiding out down there.

DAILY SUMMARY

SCOTLAND TOUR

Day Three: Inverness to Invermoriston

(50 miles; easy to moderate)

- Leave Inverness from in front of the tourist information office by heading down Church Street to the lights. Turn left here and follow the road around to the stoplight intersection.
- Go straight across on B862 toward Holm.
- Stay on the main road, *not* along the river.
- After 1½ miles, turn left at the sign to Essich.
- In almost 3 miles, take the direction toward Essich at the roundabout.
- You'll pedal through Essich 4 miles from Inverness.
- After 4 miles, take the left fork at the intersection toward Loch Duntelchaig.
- Stay on the main road after 3½ miles in Dunlichy.
- In another 2½ miles, turn right on B851.
- You'll come immediately into Invernarnie, where you turn right toward Orrogie.
- Continue on the main road through Farr and Croachy on B851.
- 3 miles outside Croachy, stay on the road toward Errogie.
- Join B862 and continue heading south.
- After 1⅓ miles, you'll ride through Errogie.

- Turn left on the B862 toward Gorthleck, which you'll reach after 1½ miles.
- After 3+ miles, following the village of Whitebridge, you'll ride uphill for about 3 miles, then downhill 5 miles into Fort Augustus.
- 6 miles from Fort Augustus, you come into Invermoriston.

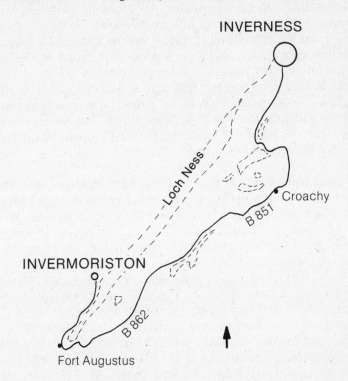

DAY FOUR: INVERMORISTON TO KYLE OF LOCHALSH

(50 miles; easy to moderate)

Another 50-mile day of the best of Scotland awaits you today. Although you'll be cycling the only access road here, you'll find it relatively lightly trafficked over moderate hills.

Head out of Invermoriston on the A887 toward Kyle of Lochalsh. The majestic terrain here rises above a roaring river as the wide road heads out of town on a slight upward slope. You'll pass a dam about 5 miles from town, with a reservoir behind it. This mountain country has acres of trees and a picturesque, meandering river valley. Almost 8 miles from Invermoriston the road narrows for a couple of miles, still sloping over long and mild hills as it follows the river valley. You'll cross a stone bridge, staying on the main road. About 10 miles into the day you'll get a good view ahead of a range of mountains that remain snowcapped most of the year. Isolated houses perch on the hillsides, and ducks gather in the shallows of the river, on your right now. The road is slightly bumpy and rolls through close trees about 13 miles into your ride. After a couple of miles the landscape opens again into smaller hills and smaller trees.

15 miles from Invermoriston take the right fork onto A87 toward Kyle of Lochalsh. The terrain becomes more rugged here, with the river on your left, and rises over moderate hills, past a large dam, and beside Loch Cluanie, leveling out to follow the edge of this long, wide loch in the moors, outcroppings, and tall mountains. Even sheep are rare out here in this wild country. The road slopes somewhat uphill in bursts, but is mostly level around the loch. The air is truly bracing: clean, bright, clear. It's very quiet, except for the birds. About 25 miles from Invermoriston is a perfect (and well-placed) lunch stop, the Cluanie Inn, where you can rest and refresh yourself in mountain splendor. The route ribbons uphill slightly past mountains, velvety with grass and moss. After 2 miles the slope levels out and moves into a section with the tall pines of the Cluanie Forest and rock cliffs on the right before turning slightly downhill. The river bubbles to your left beneath the treeless mountains. The alpine scenery here is splendid; sharply rising mountains with craggy outcroppings. Streams have made whorls and irregular patterns on the mountainsides. You'll see the thin opening of the pass down in the distance through these cloud-shadowed hills. Some 20 miles from your turn onto A87 you pass **Shiel Bridge.**

Continue on the A87 toward Kyle of Lochalsh. You'll ride around the edge of Loch Duich for several miles now, staying on the main road. Many residents make their enviable homes around the loch, where the road passes through **Inverinate,** a little less than 3 miles from Shiel Bridge. Rock outcroppings line sections of the road, which opens again on the loch past more civilization than you've passed in 30 miles—though it isn't extensive.

Approximately 7 miles from Shiel Bridge you'll see the Eileen Donan Castle on a little island connected by a bridge to the mainland. The castle was restored earlier in the century, and now two rooms are open to the public. If you walk out to the outer rampart of the castle, you can see three lochs. The castle has a perfect fairy-tale look, with its arched bridge and clustered stone buildings. Just after the castle and 7½ miles from Shiel Bridge, you'll enter **Dornie,** a lochside town with boats at the harbor. Leaving town, and a view of the loch, you pedal through more grasslands and hilly pastures, where in the season we last visited, fields of daffodils and lupine bloomed. A slight uphill takes you through hills clothed in pines. Stay on the road to Kyle, which affords intermittent views of the large loch on the last miles into Kyle. You've gone 4½ miles from Dornie when you come into **Reraig,** a village of stone houses facing the loch, which you skirt again. A short rise of about ½ mile passes a stony border cut through to make the road and descends into another glorious view of the loch. You have another steady uphill of about ¼ mile that crests to a view back over the loch and the Isle of Skye. You come into **Kyle of Lochalsh** 8 miles from Dornie.

WHERE TO STAY AND DINE IN KYLE OF LOCHALSH

Kyle of Lochalsh, in addition to having a wonderfully romantic name, is known as the jumping-off place to explore the Isle of Skye and other smaller islands. There's not a lot to see and do in Kyle of Lochalsh itself, but after a 50-mile day, you'll probably want to rest up here before heading on to the Isle of Skye.

Overlooking the village and the ferry is the large Lochalsh Hotel (Kyle of Lochalsh, Ross-shire IV40 8AB; tel. [0599]4203). Some of the interior of the hotel looks like the inside of a yacht; appropriately so, because the hotel served during World War II as a naval headquarters. This old luxury hotel commands high prices today, with a double running well over £100. (Top)

Simpler lodgings can be found at the Retreat Guest House (Main Street, Kyle of Lochalsh, Ross-shire IV40 8BY; tel. [0599]4308). In the village, this little lodging has ten or so bedrooms with bed and breakfast. (Medium)

Near Kyle of Lochalsh, in the village of Glenelg, the Eilanreach can be found (Lilliesleaf, Melrose, Roxburghshire TD6 9JG; tel. [08357]471) in a setting which served as the locale for the book *Ring of Bright Water*. There are five cottages for rent in this country setting. (Medium)

The tourist information center has many B&Bs listed, and can assist you with lodgings.

One of the best meals in Kyle of Lochalsh is served at the Highland Designworks Café, which specializes in natural foods cuisine. Their homemade soups, served with wholewheat bread, are refreshing; when possible their produce is organically grown. For light meals, their self-service counter is open until 9:30 P.M. (tel. [0599]4388).

At the railroad station the Biadh Bath Café serves good homemade garlic bread, pizza, quiches, and seafood. (Modest)

The Waverly Restaurant, also on the main street, is a good place to stop in for fresh seafood. (Low Medium)

DAILY SUMMARY

SCOTLAND TOUR

Day Four: Invermoriston to Kyle of Lochalsh

(50 miles; easy to moderate)

- Leave Invermoriston on A887 (sign: Kyle of Lochalsh).
- After 15 miles, turn on the right fork toward Kyle of Lochalsh on A87. The A87 will take you all the way to Kyle of Lochalsh.
- 25 miles from Invermoriston is the Cluanie Inn (lunch).
- Shiel Bridge is 12 miles from the Cluanie Inn.
- You'll pass through Inverinate a little less than 3 miles from Shiel Bridge.
- You can visit Eileen Donan Castle 7 miles from Shiel Bridge, and will ride through Dornie shortly thereafter.
- 4½ miles from Dornie you come through Reraig.
- In another 3½ miles you come into Kyle of Lochalsh.

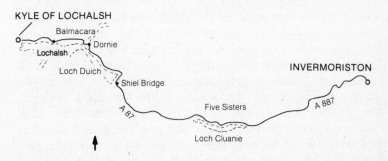

DAY FIVE: ISLE OF SKYE—KYLEAKIN TO DUNVEGAN

(48 miles; moderate to challenging)
We've toured the Isle of Skye twice, once in glorious weather and once in cold rain and cloud. Good weather is better,

although the dramatically changing weather on Skye has no doubt been a source for the Isle's mystical reputation.

The fine views begin the moment your front wheel rolls off the ferry from Kyle of Lochalsh, with the pretty little lighthouse island to your right just as you leave the village of Kyleakin. Today's 48 miles are moderate to challenging, with several long hills in the afternoon.

You are leaving town on the A850. The wide road has a mild upward incline through pine forest and water views. After 2 miles you round the bend to see the tall Cuillin Mountains and the Broadford Bay and Inner Sound opening before you. There is basically one main road around Skye; we're going to circumnavigate the Isle to the west first. Your initial route flows over small hills; the mountains and sounds spread out and disappear into the mist. (By the way, you'll see a lot of signs out here in Gaelic—nearly 60 percent of the population speaks the ancient language.)

After 6 miles, bear right on the A850 toward Portree. You'll ride through the large village of **Skulamus,** with its several B&Bs and sea-facing homes. Another mile brings you through **Broadford,** a town that combines the charm of old stone houses with modern conveniences. Crossing a bridge you come out into countryside again, where there is a fledgling pine forest. Stay on the A850. The steady but mild uphill moves through reforested areas and past the grassy island of Scalpay offshore to your right. A few sheep roam the pastures. The level road bends through several small villages and on a slight upslope for about 1½ miles. Hills and mountains rising up out of the water are quite spectacular as you turn left to follow the Loch Ainort. The little village of **Luib,** 7 miles from Broadford, has a great view of water and mountains. In Luib you may want to make a brief stop to see the nineteenth-century interior of the Old Skye Crofter's House, a thatched cottage. After you turn up the other side of Loch Ainort the road turns moderately and steadily uphill, overlooking the loch for a little under 2 miles. The view of Caol Mor over the crest here is special, with the eroded hills to

your left now on this long downhill. Rocks and heather cluster
in the moors on the hillsides. One more small hill brings you
into **Sconser,** on the shores of Loch Sligachan, where you can
take a ferry to the smaller island of Raasay. Leaving Sconser
the road's mild uphill curves back along the loch paralleling
the base of the mountains. After going 9 miles from Luib you
come to the junction of **Sligachan.** The Sligachan Hotel has
a variety of pub food for lunch.

Turn left on the A863 toward Dunvegan. There's a fairly stiff
climb for about a mile after the turn. This terrain is grassland
and moor, with only two small clusters of trees nestling
against one of the hills and valley. After the initial climb, the
road follows the side of the valley floor with just mild hills
every few miles. A stream threads through the lowlands.

**5 miles from Sligachan you continue on the A863 toward
Dunvegan.**
     Another moderate climb winds around the mountain with
the Loch Harport below for 2 miles before plateauing in grasslands and pastures. You head up again after a mile with a
glimpse of the loch through the hills. The next gentle to moderate rise is about a ½ mile. Yet another moderate climb of
a little over ½ mile does crest and actually turn downhill and
into a new view of the vivid green fingers of land pointing
into the Loch Bracadale, with several tiny islands and prom-
ontories. Stay on the A863 to follow the road up again
through **Struan** for ½ mile, less steeply for another ⅓, and
over moors on a slight hill. Another moderate hill challenges
you for a little over a mile 13 miles into this section. The view
here extends for miles up and down the western shores of
Skye. Stay on the A863 the final 1½ miles into **Dunvegan.**

WHERE TO STAY AND DINE IN DUNVEGAN

The Atholl House Hotel (Dunvegan, Isle of Skye, Inverness-
shire IV51 8WA; tel. [047022]219) is near Dunvegan Castle
(see below). It has been serving guests for over half a century.

The dining room is comfortable and serves seafood, lamb, and other traditional items. (Medium)

Near to Dunvegan, the Harlosh Hotel (tel. [047022]367) is a comfortable small hotel with seven bedrooms. It's recommendable for its views and for its cuisine, relying mainly on seafood from the local waters. (Modest–Medium)

The Old School Restaurant (Dunvegan, Isle of Skye; tel. [047022]421) has vegetarian and a children's menu in addition to traditional fare such as salmon and shellfish in its light, airy wood interior. (Modest)

One of the most pleasant B&Bs we found on Skye is "Easandubh," which translates as Black Waterfall (tel. Dunvegan 424). TV and tea and coffee facilities are in the clean rooms of this tidy home.

WHAT TO SEE AND DO IN DUNVEGAN

In addition to its exquisite natural beauty overlooking the Loch Dunvegan, this town is famous as the long-time home of the MacLeod clan. Their ancestral home, Dunvegan Castle, is ¾ mile outside of town and is now open to the public. It's a fascinating place to visit. There you can see the Dunvegan Horn, a relic of Malcolm III, chief of the clan. According to the legend, Malcolm was stealing home from an amorous visit to the wife of a neighboring nobleman when he was confronted by an enraged bull. He killed the animal with his dagger and kept one of the horns as a souvenir. To this day each male heir has to demonstrate his manliness by drinking a hornful of wine. There is also a boat trip from the castle to a seal colony. The castle grounds house a restaurant and craft shop. There are many relics of Bonnie Prince Charlie, who was smuggled to Skye by Flora MacDonald, a great Scottish heroine, after the defeat at Culloden. There is even a lock of the prince's hair preserved in a locket at the castle.

A pleasant day excursion is available to the village of Glendale out the B884. You'll see a sign on the outskirts of Dunvegan directing you. It is an easy round trip of less than

15 miles. A major reason to go to Glendale is the proliferation of craft shops, including Skye Silver, which offers unique Celtic patterns in gold and silver. There is a toy museum and a folk museum and an assortment of ventures that sell hand-knit items, pottery, and other crafts. There is also a very good restaurant there called Three Chimneys.

DAILY SUMMARY

SCOTLAND TOUR

Day Five: Isle of Skye—Kyleakin to Dunvegan

(48 miles; moderate to challenging)

- Leave Kyleakin on A850.
- After 6 miles, bear right on A850 (sign: Portree).
- Riding through Skulamus and for another mile brings you into Broadford, where you stay on A850.
- Luib appears 7 miles from Broadford.
- You'll pass through Sconser on the 9 miles from Luib to Sligachan.
- Turn left here on A863 toward Dunvegan.
- Continue on A863 toward Dunvegan at the junction in 5 miles.
- Dunvegan is approximately 15 miles from the last junction, after passing through several small villages.

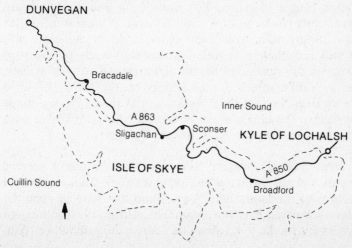

DAY SIX: ISLE OF SKYE—DUNVEGAN TO KYLEAKIN

(55 miles; moderate)

Today, the final day of this tour, takes you around more of Skye, then back to Kyle of Lochalsh. From here you can board a train to return to Inverness. In 55 miles today, your longest ride, you'll encounter more moderate hills, none of which are really steep. Some of the terrain may seem familiar as you rejoin the road back to Kyleakin.

Leave Dunvegan on the A850 toward Portree. You climb moderately through grasslands and the occasional small reforestation project for the first few miles. A little less than 4 miles after you start the road descends through grasslands, moors, and sculpted hills. The blue of a faraway loch winks at you occasionally as you come around the hills. Loch Greshorhish lies in a valley whose slopes you climb again after 2 miles. A single-track road carries you for a distance over small hills along the ridge following the loch. You'll notice that the houses on the Isle of Skye are generally small and economically built and don't tend toward frills. Dipping down into a little valley, you have a short, challenging hill to climb after another couple of miles. You crest by a line of well-established, older trees, with an unusual house in their midst. After leveling out briefly, you climb again, a longer moderate hill, but still less than a ½ mile. A downhill leads to the next inevitable upslope—this by the Treaslane River—of a little over a ½ mile. More homes appear on the shores of Loch Snizort Beag (a real mouthful) and the river. Clouds shade and pattern the hills and the faraway Cuillins are visible on a clear day. Stay on the A850 toward Portree.

16 miles from Dunvegan, turn right on the A850 toward Portree. Fenced farmland accompanies your gradual climb of a mile over moderate hills. You round the bend to view the valley of Portree between mountains. Brush and heather are often swept by the wind along this descending ribbon of road.

The roads through Skye allow long vistas through the middle of the island. You enter **Portree,** a large town where we suggest a lunch stop 3 miles after your turn.

Turn left into the town center for lunch. The beautiful setting of this town is the Sound of Raasay. There are a couple of excellent bakeries and a buffet lunch at the Collin Hills Hotel (tel. [0478]2003), which overlooks the bay. If you want to stretch your legs, there is a walk to the shore from the hotel. Our favorite restaurant, the Granary (tel. [0478]2873), was only open for dinner, but you might check to see if the policy has changed. The Rosedale Hotel (tel. [0478]2531), right on the water, is open only from the middle of May through September.

Leave Portree by turning right out of the town center and left at the junction with A850 toward Kyleakin. As you leave town the views out to Raasay are wonderful. You're pedaling along the Glen River valley over small hills and through some copses and acreage of trees. The ribbon of pavement rises on a slight to moderate grade 4½ miles out of Portree, looking as if it's heading straight into the Cuillins. You get a brief rest 2½ miles later, then encounter a series of rolling elevations past curious hillocks or bumps in the topography to our right. The Cuillins become starkly prominent 6 miles from Portree. Nine miles from Portree, in **Sligachan,** you rejoin yesterday morning's route on the A850. The difference in light, time of day, and weather can make this seem like totally new territory. As the road threads around Loch Sligachan, the view of Raasay, the Inner Sound, and Scotland beyond can be staggering on a clear day. You cover a hill and begin climbing this side of the pass after 4½ miles. From this direction the rise is steady and moderate for 2½ miles past mountain streams, mud-capped mountains, and moors of sculpted earth. The downhill from this direction is scenic and rounded, passing around the inward shores of Loch Ainort before leveling out after 1½ miles. A slight uphill curves around the edge of the loch and through **Luib,** with its white stone houses trimmed in black, a common style on Skye. You can see, looking across to Scalag, that farming and grazing occur on this smaller offshore island. **Dunan** is scattered along the shore here, followed by several small villages and stone walls. Rounding another corner you glimpse Broadford Bay before turning inland over a mostly level or downhill route for the 20 miles from Portree into **Broadford.**

The road from here back to Kyleakin rolls over a series of small hills where there are more residences as you get closer to the mainland. Flowering bushes appear and more trees. We suggest you stay in Kyleakin tonight before taking the ferry and train back to Inverness.

WHERE TO STAY AND DINE IN KYLEAKIN

Just as you come into Kyleakin you'll find one of the finest small hotels on the Isle of Skye. It's a real bargain, too. The Dunringell Hotel (Kyleakin, Isle of Skye IV41 8PR; tel. [0599]4180), is a beautiful old mansion with ten bedrooms. Set in four acres of gardens, the hotel also features a putting green and space to play croquet. (Medium)

Right in the center of Kyleakin you'll find a second option, the King's Arms Hotel (Kyleakin, Isle of Skye IV41 8PH; tel. [0599]4109), with a view of the bay and the hills in the distance. There a private bath with breakfast is also quite reasonable. (Medium)

DAILY SUMMARY

SCOTLAND TOUR

Day Six: Isle of Skye—Dunvegan to Kyleakin

(55 miles; moderate)

- Leave Dunvegan on A850 toward Portree. The A850 will be your route all the way back to Kyleakin.
- After 16 miles, turn right at the junction to stay on A850.
- In another 3 miles you'll come into Portree (lunch).

- Leave Portree by turning right out of the town center and left at the junction with A850 toward Kyleakin.
- After another 9 miles you'll pass through Sligachan.
- In 20 more miles you'll ride into Broadford, and in another 8, Kyleakin.

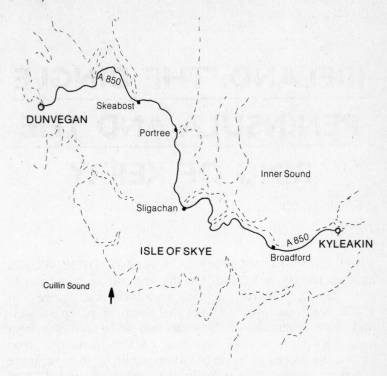

IRELAND: THE DINGLE PENINSULA AND THE RING OF KERRY

WILD COUNTRY, WONDERFUL CYCLING. THESE WORDS sum up touring in Ireland. On the tour we have laid out in this chapter, you will roll past mountains that plunge into placid bays, sheep-dotted hills that seem to go up forever, and places where the crashing surf will be 10 feet away from a pastoral view of cows munching on that incredibly green grass. The greens of Ireland fall very easily on the eye; there are more shades of it than we ever imagined existed. And despite what you may have heard about the weather, the temperature in the two areas we describe is surprisingly mild. The best reason to tour Ireland, however, is the people. They are so funny, so warm and unusual that we began to look forward to our interactions with them as one of the chief features of our day. Practically every Irish person speaks with a poetic turn of phrase, as well as the beautiful lilt of a brogue. You will hear the language spoken in a way that is not heard elsewhere.

For years before we first toured Ireland we made a practice of asking people who had just returned where their favorite places were to cycle. Nearly everyone mentioned two places, the Dingle Peninsula and the Ring of Kerry. Finally in 1990 we were able to embark on a major tour of the Emerald Isle, and sure enough, our friends had been right. The Dingle Peninsula is a place to fall in love with, not simply to visit. And the Ring of Kerry is nonstop spectacular bicycle touring. There is not a dull view in any direction.

We recommend doing the Dingle and the Ring as one tour, partly because they are linked together geographically and partly because they have a cultural similarity that deserves a bit of time and careful attention. Spending the week that it will take you to cycle through these areas will give you a chance to immerse yourself in a rich heritage. Both the Dingle and the Ring have an easy pace of life that even the tourist crowds have not unsettled. Here, perhaps more than any place we've been in Europe, there is always time for the unhurried conversation with a villager or a leisurely evening with the locals at a friendly pub. The quiet charm of these two areas, and their glorious physical beauty, will remain with us throughout our lives.

Ireland in general, like the rest of the British Isles, is perfect for cycling, save for the occasional encounter with the elements. As William Makepeace Thackeray put it one hundred and fifty years ago, "No man can speculate on Irish weather. I have seen a day beginning with torrents of rain that looked as if a deluge was on hand clear up in a few minutes . . . In like manner, after an astonishingly fine night, there came a villainous dark day." The weather has not changed or improved much since Thackeray was here. Get the best raingear you can afford, and don't let the weather stop you. The time of your visit, however, is something over which you have more control. If you pick your time for touring carefully, you can have many of the roads to yourself. This point bears emphasis, because Ireland does not have the rich network of back roads that crisscross, say, France. Often there is only one way to get to a place, where in other parts of Europe you may have a choice of many routes. Rural Ireland is more like a Third World country in this respect. This

means that you will have to share the one road with whoever
wants to drive on it. In July and August practically everybody
will want to drive on it, including the vacationing Irish, as
well as their cousins from the colonies. The roads are quite
narrow here (it is common to see two cars slowing down to
edge past each other on a road that is only built for one).
Even though drivers here are respectful of cyclists, they are,
quite frankly, the worst drivers we've seen in Europe. It's
best to take advantage of the numbers and plan your trip
when you can count on little traffic. The months of May,
June, and September will place you at good advantage. If
you can only come at peak season, however, you must be
watchful.

You must also book early if you come in July and August. Even the tiniest B&Bs tend to fill up during these
months. On our 1990 tour we made no reservations and never
needed one—but we came in May and were gone by mid-
June. We made a practice of asking wherever we stopped
whether we would need reservations if we came back in July,
and mostly got grave nods.

GETTING STARTED ON THE TOUR

The tour starts in Tralee (accent on the second syllable: truh-
lee). The best way to get to there is to fly into Shannon, not
Dublin. Shannon Airport is one of the largest airports in the
country; there are many flights daily from London and other
cities in the British Isles. From the airport it is a very pleasant
15-mile ride into Limerick. There is a wide, paved shoulder
along the road, with clearly marked signs showing you how
to get into Limerick. You'll be in good company along this
road, because the majority of young people, and a substantial
number of their elders, ride bikes as their primary form of
transportation. If you get rained out and want to take a bus,
you can catch one at the airport that will take you to the
railroad station in Limerick.

Castle enthusiasts, take note: If you are burning to see
an Irish castle, there is the splendidly restored Bunratty Castle

along the road into Limerick from the airport. You can tour a working exhibit of arts and crafts from early Irish life on the castle grounds.

There is a bicycle shop in Limerick where you can get any equipment you need or have any plane-induced traumas to your bike straightened out. If you are not too jet-lagged, catch the next train or bus for Tralee, rather than cycling. It's about an 80-mile trip down, and while the road to Tralee goes through mainly basic Irish pastoral countryside, it is quite heavily trafficked. We recommend saving your legs and eyes for the feast that awaits you in the Dingle Peninsula and the Ring of Kerry. If you do decide you want to cycle to Tralee, head on the N69 and the T68 to Tarbert, then ride to Listowell and on into Tralee. It will take you one very long or two modest days to get there.

One of the first things you will notice is that many of the road signs are written in both English and Gaelic. Sometimes out in the country they are only in Gaelic. Many of the good maps of the area have both languages, so we did not have any trouble finding our way around. Likewise, distances are often given in both miles and kilometers, though with typical Irish charm, sometimes one or the other is used with no seemingly obvious reason. Throughout this tour, distances are given in miles.

WHERE TO STAY AND DINE IN TRALEE

It appears that many Irish families are supplementing their incomes by opening their homes as bed and breakfasts, so there is no shortage of choice.

We really enjoyed the Gables, run by Mrs. Kate Nealon and ably assisted by her daughter (Listowel Road; tel. [066]24396). Our large, quiet, high-ceiled and wood-paneled room, with private bathroom and shower, had a large picture window opening on the profusely flowering backyard which adjoins a local park. Breakfast was abundant and served in the comfortable lounge. Mrs. Nealon was graciously helpful with directions and lodging suggestions. (Modest)

Two other bed and breakfast homes out of the bustle of central Tralee are the Seaview House (The Spa, Tralee; tel. [066]36107), a gorgeous Georgian house on forestland with nearby water sports and golf (Modest), and the Knockanish House (The Spa, Tralee; tel. [066]36268), which overlooks Tralee Bay and is near several seafood restaurants. (Modest)

If you prefer closer neighbors, The Grand Hotel (Denny St., Tralee; tel. [066]21499) has spacious rooms with TV, video, and radio channels. Their two dining rooms serve a variety of fresh fish and meat entrees. (Modest)

One family restaurant in central Tralee, the Allegro Restaurant (Denny and Castle streets; tel. [066]22704) serves a delicious leek soup, along with a large selection of cosmopolitan dishes, a four-course meal, and several vegetable and salad selections. (Modest)

WHAT TO SEE AND DO IN AND AROUND TRALEE

Tralee is the site of both the Rose of Tralee International Festival, a spirited and parade-enhanced beauty pageant, and the Folk Festival of Ireland; both occur at the same time in late August and early September. Accommodations anywhere in this popular area are especially coveted at this time, so advance booking is strongly recommended.

Fenit Castle stands on Fenit Island, 2 miles from the village, and was originally constructed to overlook and protect the busy harbor. A morning's ride from Tralee to Castleisland (11 miles) brings you to Crag Cave, one of the longest cave structures in Ireland and only recently discovered. Full of large chambers and extensive stalagtite and stalagmite formations, the 12,000 feet or more of the cave is specially lighted and several chambers are named for various characters in Tolkien's mythology, such as Balrog's Bathtub and PollNa Gollum.

DAY ONE: TRALEE TO DINGLE

(42 miles; moderate to challenging)
Our first, 42-mile day introduces you to this magnificent land through a gentle morning ride and fairly strenuous afternoon climb over the Slieve Mish Mountains to Dingle. This land is to be savored, not rushed through. Chances are you won't need to rush through, anyway, because the days in summer are very long, not darkening until after 10 P.M. Many people consider the Dingle Peninsula one of the most beautiful places on earth. As the quick-changing weather alters the landscape, you'll be enchanted by the nuances of color and tone.

Begin in the center of town at the tourist office on Denny Street. Turn right and follow the signs that say Dingle on the R559.

At the stop sign just out of town, turn right. (sign: Dingle) You'll be riding out through flat farmland, with a bike trail at points along the left side of the road. We found the trail fine for mountain bikes but probably a little too rough for thin-tired bicycles. As you head toward Blennerville, you'll see looming mountains far off to your left. After about a mile you'll pass over a bridge into **Blennerville,** the site of a much-visited windmill (and coffee shop). It is currently being restored as Ireland's only commercially operated windmill, complete with demonstrations when the weather permits.

Outside Blennerville you can pick up the bike path again, but soon the road narrows, passing through hedge-lined fields over gently undulating hills. There are lots of B&Bs along the road, many of them tempting. There don't seem to be any back roads out of Tralee, but we found motorists accommodating, if somewhat erratic. About a mile or two outside of Blennerville the bay opens to your right.

The road climbs a little and wends its way through small farms, each neatly separated by ancient, moss-covered stone fences and hedges. The Slieve Mish Mountains rise to your left and spill into Tralee Bay on your right.

When the road forks about 9 miles from Tralee, take the right fork toward Conor Pass. As soon as you take this fork, the true beauty of the Dingle Peninsula blooms. You'll cycle along a narrow road flanked by hedgerows of profuse growth, high and low. It's worth a frequent stop to admire the scenery at breaks in the rows, as they are generally just high enough to obscure your view as you ride. Passing through a residential area and sheep farms, stay on the main road, which is basically level.

After 5 miles, take a right on R560 at the fork to visit Castlegregory Village and Rough Point at land's end. (sign: Maharees Peninsula) We recommend this 10-mile round-trip detour to see a part of the Dingle Peninsula that many people flash by without sampling its rural charm. This finger of land separates Tralee Bay from Brandon Bay. Along the way you'll roll along a pretty road lined with berry bushes. You'll pass through the little village of Castlegregory after about a mile.

At the three-pronged fork, take the middle path. (signs: Fahamore, Kilshannig) The landscape becomes more austere, with grass-covered dunes rising above the bay, dotted with daffodil fields and an occasional stream. You may share the road with an errant horse or casual cows out selecting edibles. The road winds just above the bay for a bracing stretch.

At the fork, go right toward Kilshannig. You'll ride through more dunes and by frisky horses into the tiny village of **Kilshannig** at land's end. There's a beach if you're inclined to stroll. When you're ready, return along the same road, passing a waterfowl sanctuary before coming to **Castelgregory.**

Take the right fork here. (sign: Conor Pass 10¼) This very pretty section of the ride passes old stone houses, sheep-filled meadows, and flocks of birds floating on the winds along the bay. At the T fork go right toward Conor Pass. The multihued fields take you shortly into **Stradbally,** where we recommend you stop for lunch at the little bar and tea shop. As you climb a gentle hill outside Stradbally you'll have a beautiful view of the Brandon Valley and a pristine beach to your right.

After 2 miles, at the junction in **Kilcummin,** you can take a side trip out to Brandon point (20 miles, round-trip), or you can head on toward Dingle Town, still a stiff 15-mile ride.

If you head on toward Dingle, the road first goes downhill through more tree-dotted territory, then turns over a bridge and more gently uphill through a steady progression of small homes and fuchsia bush–lined roads. After about a mile you leave the heavy foliage and move into grazing land. The road turns at first moderately and then steeply uphill, with a lush valley on your right. Gray mottled rock and heathery moss landscape appear as the road narrows, with a rock wall protecting you from a drop on the right. The climb to the top of Conor Pass is about 2½ miles; the views from the top are exquisite. You will probably want to stop often for a rest, but even if you are not tired you may have to stop anyway from time to time to let cars pass on this very narrow road. After the viewing area at the summit, the rock wall moves to your left as you descend into the valley. As we crested the summit we were enveloped in thick fog. As you cruise downhill, bushes and hedges reappear, as do fields of sheep and meadows.

It's about a 5-mile ride on into **Dingle,** a bustling harbor town and a major tourist destination. The more charming area of Dingle Town is down by the water. You will find the tourist information office on the main street, with a bike shop that's open daily just around the corner.

WHERE TO STAY AND DINE IN DINGLE

Our plan calls for staying here two nights, returning to Dingle after the second day's ride around the peninsula. There is a huge variety of bed and breakfast establishments available in Dingle. We can personally recommend two, and the tourist information office can help you if those are full.

The Dingle Heights B&B is excellent (Ballinboola, Dingle; tel. [066]51543) and has a superb view of the harbor. (Modest)

The Greenmount House (Gortanora, Dingle; tel. [066]51414) boasts orthopedic beds and is in a quiet location. (Modest)

Two B&Bs with sea views are a few miles outside of town toward Ventry. Mrs. Kennedy runs Clooneevin (tel. [066]59916), and the Ballymore House is operated by Mrs. Birmingham (tel. [066]59050).

If you want the ambience of a larger hotel, several are located in the downtown area.

Doyle's Seafood Bar and Townhouse (tel. [066]51174) offers perhaps the finest table in town. The food is fresh (often having spent the morning in Dingle Bay). (Modest)

Connor's Dingle Bay Restaurant (tel. [066]51598), on Dykegate Street, is a family-run establishment that features fresh Dingle Bay prawns, sea trout, and lobster. They are also well known for their desserts. (Medium)

DAILY SUMMARY

IRELAND TOUR

Day One: Tralee to Dingle

(42 miles; moderate to challenging)

- From the tourist office on Denny Street, turn right on the R559 (sign: Dingle).
- Turn right at the stop sign just out of town.
- 9 miles from Tralee, take the right fork toward Conor Pass.
- In 5 more miles, turn right on R560 (sign: Maharees Peninsula). This loop is 10 miles.
- At the 3-pronged fork, take the middle path.
- At the next fork, go right toward Kilshannig.
- Retrace your path to Castlegregory.
- Take the right fork here (sign: Conor Pass).
- Follow the signs to Dingle up over the pass.
- After the pass you have about 5 miles into Dingle.

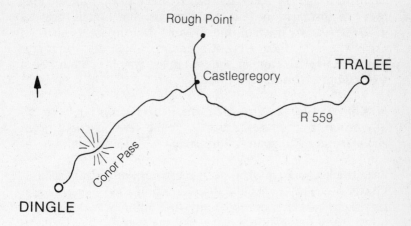

DAY TWO: THE DINGLE LOOP

(26 miles; moderate)
The purpose of today's 26-mile loop to Slea Head and back
is to view firsthand the westernmost part of Europe, a wild
and spectacular part of the peninsula. Don't worry about getting lost. Often in Ireland we'd be standing with a map in hand,
and always a local would initiate a query, "Will you be needing
anything?" One very pleasant-voiced man offered to lead us to
our next stop. Your whole tour (except for the Gallarus loop)
today will be on the R559, and you'll notice that the Irish prefer
place names to numbers, which you will rarely see.

**Begin today's tour on the western side of Dingle, taking the
road straight across the junction at the sign for Ballyferriter.**

Very shortly you'll encounter another sign where you'll turn right.
(sign: Ballydavid) This straight, level road passes through farmland. After about 1½ miles, the grade turns slightly uphill. After
going 5 miles from Dingle you'll crest this section.

**At the three-pronged fork with many signs, take the middle
road (straight).** (signs: An Doneen, M.D. Gearailt) You'll

curve downhill all the way into a gorgeous valley stretching into the distance. A mile past the last junction is a metal gate with early Christian ruins beyond. Shortly after this is an excavation site, then a twelfth-century church on your right, the Kilmalkedar Romanesque Church, which contains both Celtic and romanesque artifacts.

In **Kilmalkedar** (a little past these sights), turn left at the X junction, and left again shortly, at the next junction. (sign: Ballyferriter) The road is very level over the next mile.

Take the left fork (straight) at the next junction. (sign: Gallarus Oratory—we saw it spelled three different ways) The grade is first slightly, then more moderately, and finally steeply uphill. After just a few hundred feet you'll see signs for the Gallarus Oratory, an eighth-century Christian relic oratory, the only perfect remaining example of its type, a watertight structure without mortar which resembles an overturned boat. After you climb you'll come to a junction where you rejoin the main road, just a little below the many-signed junction you took to make this little loop-within-a-loop.

Turn right (unmarked). You now glide downhill past velvety hills to your left, then level along flower-lined fields.

After 3 miles, turn left. (sign: Ballyferriter)

After 100 yards or so, go right. (sign: Baile an Fheirtearaigh) The level road leads into **Ballyferriter,** which houses a church, a heritage center, and a wonderful hotel, the Ostan Granville. The road from here can be bumpy, and bracing winds may accompany you out to the edge of the peninsula.

At the next junction, go straight, staying on the main road. Your route is mainly level and downhill into a tiny village, then slightly uphill as the peninsula unfolds on either side. After a pottery studio you'll lean into a moderate uphill out to the cliffs. We took, and recommend, a hike here to more closely experience the beauty of the views looking out to sea

and back over the hills and fertile valley of the Dingle Peninsula. Due to patterns of light and the rapidly changing
weather, the scenery looks different with each turn. After this
turn in the road, the road winds down into **Dunquin** (4½ miles
from Ballyferriter). On the edge of town is a lounge where
you may want to have coffee or lunch.

At the next junction, turn right. (sign: Dunquin pottery and
café) The road turns up- and downhill now past cattle and
horses munching lazily. (Note to coffee lovers: There is a
pottery shop and café just past Dunquin that serves delicious,
fresh-brewed coffee with rich, thick cream.) One moderate
uphill completes the slightly more than 2½ miles into **Slea
Head,** which divides its land with lots of stark stone walls,
rather than the grass-covered walls you have seen so far. The
spring-green hills are dazzling in the sun. A stone wall on your
right separates the very narrow road from the cliff's edge, but
doesn't impede the breathtaking views everywhere, over
water to the Blasket Islands, past home of famous storytellers,
or up to the jutting rocks on your left. About 1½ miles past
Slea Head are the Beehive Huts on your left, prehistoric
dwellings of stone. About ¼ mile farther, you'll turn a corner
over a running streambed in the road.

You'll meet many cyclists on this tour, which is very popular. As you pedal along the coast back to Dingle, the view
is across Dingle Bay to your future ride, the Ring of Kerry.

After more stone walls the road levels and then turns
downhill the last few hundred feet into **Ventry** (5½ miles from
Slea Head). The vegetation becomes more profuse again here,
with fuchsia bushes and deeper growth reappearing. Stay on
the main road, slightly uphill, past the church in Ventry. The
shoreline opens up on your right, where windsurfers were
heading. The road passes open fields and grasslands, and another pottery studio, as it follows the coastline, slightly up
and down for several miles, then turns inland toward Dingle.
Downhill and level, you'll feel the shadow of a tree canopy
under the dappled sun before climbing two slight hills, crossing a bridge, and turning right to follow the main road. About
5½ miles from Ventry, you reenter **Dingle.**

DAILY SUMMARY

IRELAND TOUR

Day Two: The Dingle Loop

(26 miles; moderate)

- At the western end of Dingle, take the road straight across the junction at the sign for Ballyferriter.
- Turn right very shortly at the next sign (Ballydavid).
- After 5 miles, take the middle fork at the 3-fork intersection (signs: An Doneen, M.D. Gearailt).
- In Kilmalkedar, a little over a mile farther, turn left at the X junction, and again left at the next junction (sign: Ballyferriter).
- After a mile, take the left fork (sign: Gallarus Oratory).
- Turn right at the top of the hill (unmarked).
- After 3 miles, turn left (sign: Ballyferriter).
- After 100 yards or so, turn right (sign: Baile an Fheirtearaigh).
- After Ballyferriter, go straight, staying on the main road.
- After Dunquin, 4½ miles from Ballyferriter, turn right (sign: Dunquin pottery and café).
- You'll remain on this main road a little more than 2½ miles through Slea Head, 5½ miles into Ventry, and the final 5½ miles back into Dingle.

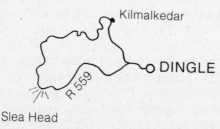

DAY THREE: DINGLE TO GLENBEIGH

(42 miles; moderate)

On this day we make the transition from one peninsula to another: from Dingle Peninsula to the Ring of Kerry. This

42-mile day combines rolling hills and coastal views through a constantly changing landscape.

Exit the eastern end of Dingle on the lower road. You'll be heading toward Annascaul. Your first mile of gentle ups and downs passes through farmlands and opens up into a deeper valley where you can see farther than the hedgerows have often allowed. The road is a little wider and straighter, and the Slieve Mish mountains are now to your left. You'll ride through **Lispole** 5 miles from Dingle.

The grade becomes steeper here as you ride through more agricultural land. For alternate miles you'll first glide downhill then go uphill before turning the corner into a great view out to sea and the peninsula of the Ring of Kerry. The road next turns very windy and downhill. Stop occasionally for a spectacular look over your shoulder back out to sea.

About 5 miles from Lispole, at the Y junction, go right. (signs: Castlemaine, Killarney) Follow the signs to Castlemaine, downhill through rolling hills for less than a mile, then steadily up again as the road widens, coming out onto the bay. The road widens and narrows as you follow the coastline, with slight hills. There are very few people in this area; it has a wild and desolate look. We suggest stopping in **Inch** for lunch at the pub. This lunch stop is about 14 miles from Dingle. Afterward, stay on the main road up and down the gentle hills through a residential area with the bay to your right. After 3 miles you'll pass through **Waterside.** The road levels out then goes up and down again after a mile. Follow the signs to Castlemaine, through this more residential area. After 8 miles you pass through **Boolteens,** where the road is straight and fairly level. Houses line the road at regular intervals. Another 2 miles bring you into **Castlemaine,** whose name derives from its former use as a fortress for the once-busy port.

Turn right on N70 (sign: Killarney)

Take another right on N70 in just 100 yards. This lightly trafficked road leads you in 2 miles into the busy little town of **Milltown.** Be alert here, because the signs are confusing.

Turn right at the sign to Killagh Priory. (There are many confusing signs on left side of the street, but the sign to Killagh Priory is on the right side of the street.) You'll have a fairly steep climb out of town then gently rolling hills that are lined with heavy hedges. After 4 miles you'll approach the outskirts of Killorglin.

Go right over the bridge into Killorglin. (sign: Glencar)

Just as you enter town turn right at the sign to Glenbeigh.

Follow the signs to Glenbeigh past a large church on your right and the tourist information bureau. The scenery that brings people from all over the world to the Ring of Kerry starts a couple of miles outside Killorglin. Caragh Lake is a good side trip a few miles past Killorglin. Watch for the sign on the left directing you to the lake, which is just a mile or so off the main road.

6 miles outside Killorglin turn right at the sign to Glenbeigh. Continue following the signs to town past the river and the ancient ruins of a bridge. A left over another bridge brings you into **Glenbeigh.**

 Glenbeigh is on the edge of a mountain area, where the pines and tall trees sing in the wind. Killorglin is a busy and rather ugly town, and we enjoyed staying out in this more pristine setting.

WHERE TO STAY AND DINE IN GLENBEIGH

The best-looking B&B is the Ocean Wave, operated by Mrs. Noreen O'Toole (tel. [066]68249). This spacious well-furnished home has a good view of the bay. (Modest)

 The Glenbeigh Hotel (tel. [066]68333), a pretty white

building with iron trim, has modest, simply-furnished rooms and a thriving restaurant. (Modest)

The quietest setting belongs to the Falcon Inn Hotel (tel. [066]68215), situated just in front of a wooded mountain a mile past Glenbeigh. The large public rooms are very friendly, and the bedrooms are small but very clean. (Medium)

DAILY SUMMARY

IRELAND TOUR

Day Three: Dingle to Glenbeigh

(42 miles; moderate)

- Leave Dingle at its eastern side on the lower road, heading toward Annascaul.
- 5 miles take you into Lispole.
- 5 miles from Lispole, go right at the Y junction (signs: Castlemaine, Killarney).
- Waterside is 3 miles farther.
- 2 more miles lead you into Castlemaine.
- Turn right on N70 (sign: Killarney).
- Turn right again on the N70 in 100 yards.
- Turn right at the sign to Killagh Priory in the middle of town.
- Killorglin is 4 miles farther.
- Turn right just as you enter town (sign: Glenbeigh).

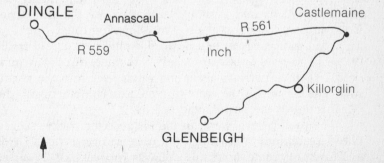

- Follow the signs to Glenbeigh past a large church on your right.
- Turn right at the sign to Glenbeigh 6 miles outside Killorglin.

DAY FOUR: GLENBEIGH TO WATERVILLE

(48 miles; challenging)
Today's 48-mile jaunt is the toughest one on the tour, but certainly one of the most rewarding. You will travel through territory that is the essence of what bicycle touring is all about. After beginning on the tourist circuit (because that's where some of the beauties of this region are to be found), you will strike out through a remote area that few tourists brave. You will also encounter a hill along the way that will challenge your legs and your good humor.

Continue on the main road through Glenbeigh.

Just outside of town follow the signs to Waterville to your left.
A thickly-forested pine mountain rises to your right as you ride into an area rich with streams and long valleys. The road inclines first slightly then moderately uphill for 4 miles. You'll then pass through some moderately high rock cliffs and down into a great view of Dingle Bay. Here you can see farther than anywhere else on the tour. The road here along the coastline widens and a shoulder appears for the first time. You can now see across the bay to where you rode yesterday. The road soon narrows and heads downhill past an old trellis bridge. The road swells to include a shoulder for a few hundred feet, then narrows again and winds back into the peninsula. The air carries the scent of the ocean combined with the sweet smell of the pastureland nearby.

The road is level here; in the distance the rocky, rugged hills descend into farmland as you traverse this section. Fields and forest alternate along this valley as you roll past flowering bushes and tree windbreaks.

At a junction 14 miles from Glenbeigh, follow the Ring of Kerry sign. The Doulus Bay appears on your right as the road grade goes slightly uphill. In a couple of miles you will come into **Cahersiveen.** You climb up into the town, where you might refresh yourself at the outdoor fruit market, open throughout the warmer season. There is a pretty church here that may interest you; the combination art gallery and coffee shop is worth a stop; and there are several shops where you can get picnic supplies. It's a good idea to pack a lunch before setting off on the next section, because you will be going out to a remote region where there are few amenities.

3 miles out of town turn right on R565. (signs: St. Finian's Bay, Valentia)

In approximately a mile turn right at the Y fork. (sign: Portmagee) The land you are now entering has the magic feel of Ireland. It is sparse, windblown, and hardly inhabited. The road goes uphill then levels out through farmland, with the Portmagee Channel on your right. A few slight hills cover the 6 miles to your next junction.

Turn right at the sign to **Portmagee** and ride into town.

Take a left at the sign for St. Finian's Bay, taking you past the little harbor of this small village.

Very shortly, take another left at the corner with the sign for St. Finian's Bay.

In less than 100 feet, turn right at the Skellig Ring sign. As soon as you turn, you'll see a ribbon of road rising up into the sky. This is the big hill we mentioned earlier. Although it is only a mile to the top, it seems eternal. Then again, the 2-mile ride down the other side is breathtaking, both in steepness and scenery.

At the summit of the hill, follow the sign to St. Finian's Bay.

Along the downhill run, follow the Skellig Ring signs. On the day we did this loop we saw an equal number of cyclists and cars, four of each.

The village at St. Finian's Bay is unmarked. As you leave it you will have a steady uphill climb for 2 miles. The land is rockier here, with the grazing land working a little harder for its purchase on these hills. As you crest the hill, sweeping views open out over Ballinskelligs Bay.

Turn right at the An Coirnean sign, then left at the same sign at the bottom of the hill. In **Ballinskelligs,** reached within a mile, there's a large beer garden inn and restaurant for afternoon refreshments.

After about ½ mile, go straight at the sign to Cahersiveen.

Turn right at the sign to Waterville after another 1½ miles. A long beach with rolling surf appears to your right as the road levels out and rolls through lowlands with small stands of pine and other trees. After about 3 miles you have one last short climb to rejoin the main Ring of Kerry road.

Turn right on N70. (signs: Kenmare, Waterville)

After approximately 1 mile take a right at the sign to Waterville. You'll pass more fields of flowers on an open road where oncoming traffic is visible. Within a mile you enter **Waterville.**

WHERE TO STAY AND DINE IN WATERVILLE

As you come into Waterville, there is a pleasant little bed and breakfast called The Forge (tel. [0667]4136). If you're about to drop from the day's cycling, turn in here. (Modest)

Further on, in the small heart of Waterville, is a grander option, the Butler Arms Hotel (tel. [0667]4144), with large rooms, often facing the sea. (Medium)

On the way out of Waterville, there is a beautiful country lane, Lake Road, that leads about a mile (don't give up) to a bed and breakfast called Lakelands House (tel. [0667]4303), overlooking the large and sparkling Lough Currane. (Medium)

The best meal to be had in town is at the Butler Arms, but the price is steep. (Medium)

Two other options are The Huntsman and the Sheilin Seafood Restaurant, both of which serve fresh seafood from local waters. (Medium) Central Waterville has a 2-block seafront section, then dissolves into stone-walled fields and marshland.

DAILY SUMMARY

IRELAND TOUR

Day Four: Glenbeigh to Waterville

(48 miles; challenging)

- Continue on the main road through Glenbeigh (the N70).
- Follow the signs left to Waterville just outside town.
- 14 miles from Glenbeigh, follow the Ring of Kerry sign.
- 2 miles or so bring you into Cahersiveen.
- 3 miles farther, turn right on R565 (signs: St. Finian's Bay, Valentia.
- After about a mile, turn right at the Y fork (sign: Portmagee).
- Turn right at the sign to Portmagee and ride through town.
- Take a left at the sign for St. Finian's Bay.
- Very shortly, turn left again at the corner (sign: St. Finian's Bay).
- In less that 100 feet, turn right (sign: Skellig Ring).
- At the summit of the mile-long steep hill, follow the sign to St. Finian's Bay.
- Along the downhill, follow the Skellig Ring signs.
- 2 miles after the unmarked village of St. Finian's Bay, go right at the An Coirnean sign, then left at the same sign at the bottom of the hill.
- You'll reach Ballinskelligs within a mile.
- After another ½ mile, go straight at the sign to Cahersiveen.
- Head right after 1½ miles (sign: Waterville).

- After a little over 3 miles, turn right on N70 (signs: Waterville, Kenmare).
- In another mile, take a right at the sign to Waterville, which you'll enter within another mile.

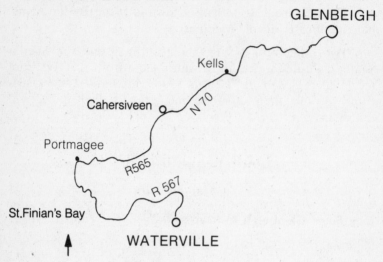

DAY FIVE: WATERVILLE TO KENMARE

(38 miles; moderate)
Today's 38-mile ride is what the phrase "unsurpassed beauty" was invented to describe. Every turn in the road brings visual pleasure in a ride that encompasses both seashore and rugged mountain terrain. After your initial steady climb, most of the road has low hills or level terrain. You'll end the day in the exquisitely cosmopolitan town of Kenmare, whose buildings and streets resemble a European or Swiss village.

Leave Waterville south on the N70 toward Kenmare. The road has a slight upgrade as you pedal the winding road past low stone walls and long fields. As you follow the road around the coastline of Hogshead you'll see farms spread out below your route right up to the edge of the cliffs. The hills are rugged, with gray boulders, as you begin a mile-long moderate upgrade through Coomakesta Pass. The landscape is desolate and windblown until you cross the summit, where a panoramic view of Kenmare River (as large as a bay) and the islands that dot the ocean greet you. A little inn at the top stocks food and great views. The rock-strewn hills tumble down into the bay with a tiny village at the edge of the water.

The road levels out here, 5 miles into your ride, as flowering rhododendrons appear. The profusion of trees on a jutting promontory below are part of Derryname National Historic Park. The road then turns downhill into the very pretty little village of **Caherdaniel.** The old stone buildings and fields are scattered over ridges and rolling hills. You may want to stop and walk around a bit to admire this little jewel more closely. Next on your route are a few small hills as the road continues to follow the coastline. Several beaches may tempt you to stop and wet your feet in the sand. The road continues to roll up and down little hills as you pass the Kerry Way Walking Route about 12 miles into your ride. On overcast days the top of Eagles Hill to your left is shrouded in mist, adding to the forlorn and undoubtedly poetically inspiring quality of this area. You'll pass several ancient houses by the side of the road, their stones rounded with age and covered with lichen and moss. The air is an incredibly fragrant combination of pine, sea, and wildflower.

Out of nowhere as you round a turn after 3 miles is the Brambles coffee shop in a charming little house, with tables out under the trees. The narrow road is basically level here, with more spectacular vistas at each bend in the road. Fairly straight for a stretch after 2 more miles, the road begins to rise a little and wind the 5 miles into Sneem. You'll see more vivid pink wild rhododendrons lining the road. The hills rise higher on the left. They call these mountains; being from Colorado, we would call them hills, but they are quite striking. The road presents you with a series of little hiccuping hills as you ride into the winner of Ireland's Tidy Town Award, **Sneem.** This village, which boasts two landscaped town squares and some of the first flowers and trimmed hedges we

saw, is a perfect lunch stop. You can choose from O'Sullivan's
for both scones and seafood, the pretty Village Kitchen, or a
variety of other shops.

**Right outside town, take the Ring of Kerry Road right, toward
Kenmare.** You climb two small hills exiting Sneem, then basically pedal through level terrain. A luscious forest walk appears, 2 miles outside Sneem, followed by a golf course on
your right. An abundance of huge rhododendron bushes hang
over the road. Then the land becomes forested as you roll
through gentle hills and catch peeks of the water through the
trees. The road opens again and is lined with ferns and trees.
Keep following the main road. After about 3 miles Tahilla
Cove, a small body of water among the rocky hills, opens to
your left for a short view. Low shrubs and moss-covered rocks
enhance the mysterious quality of this area.

In 2 more miles the Kenmare River is visible again over
the rock wall as you follow the coastline. Then you plunge
into a forest of taller and thicker trees.

**At the junction 2 miles farther, follow the signs to Kenmare
and the Ring of Kerry.** The road is slightly uphill here, then
rolls into gentle up- and downhill for a couple of miles, with
a flash of Kenmare River and then more forest, with wild
flowers and ferns perfuming the air. There is a hiking trail
here leading down to the Kenmare River, then some ancient
church ruins. You'll approach the outskirts of Kenmare
through the unmarked town of **Reem** and a more residential
area, with houses dotting the forest and fields for the remaining 3 miles into **Kenmare.**

WHERE TO STAY AND DINE IN KENMARE

If you haven't been bitten by the shopping bug on this tour,
Kenmare may tempt you. Small, prosperous shops offer a
variety of woolen goods and other Irish specialties. The bed
and breakfast establishments here are tremendously enhanced
by the local beauty, and there are several great ones from
which to choose.

The Muxnaw Lodge (tel. [064]41252) is a large converted nineteenth-century residence that looks over Kenmare Bay. Three of the five bedrooms have their own bathrooms, and there is a tennis court if you are packing your racquet. (Modest–Medium)

The lovely nineteenth-century Rose Cottage (tel. [064]41330) is run by Mrs. Murphy. It has four bedrooms, its own private gardens, and is in town. (Modest)

The Mountain View (tel. [064]41394) offers homemade baked goods and fresh garden produce. It has three bedrooms and is about 5 miles outside of town. (Modest)

Light, tasty meals are available from Mickey Ned's Coffee Shop, which has an informal atmosphere and a good selection of sandwiches and baked goods. (Modest)

If you are in the mood for something fancier, the Lime Tree Restaurant serves seafood and Irish specialties. It is only open for dinner. (Medium)

There are a dozen other restaurants and bars that we didn't get a chance to explore, but which looked promising.

A DAY TRIP FROM KENMARE

If you have fallen in love with this region, you might want to spend an extra day or two here. If so, there is another ride that could provide a fine day of cycling. It is a 54-mile loop that heads through two mountain passes and takes you onto the Beara Peninsula. You head south out of town over the suspension bridge and turn onto the Bantry/Glengarriff road (T65/N71). There is a gentle climb to begin with, for about 8 miles, then a serious climb to the Tunnels for the next few miles. An exhilarating downhill run of 6 miles will definitely clear your mind of other thoughts for its duration. At **Glengariff,** head toward Adrigole and Castletown Bere. Past the post office a ½ mile or so, you cross a bridge and then turn off the main road toward the Healy Pass. There is another heroic climb of nearly 5 miles to the top, then a descent of 4 miles to **Lauragh.** Head right over the bridge, then shortly take a left. A couple of hundred yards farther, take the right toward Kilmackillogue. From here follow the coast road which will bring you back to the main road and Kenmare.

DAILY SUMMARY

IRELAND TOUR

Day Five: Waterville to Kenmare

(38 miles; moderate)

- Leave Waterville south on the N70 toward Kenmare. This main road is your basic route through the day.
- After about 5 miles you'll ride through Caherdaniel.
- Sneem is 13½ miles from Caherdaniel.
- Right outside town, take the Ring of Kerry Road right, toward Kenmare.
- At the junction 2 miles farther, follow the signs to Kenmare and the Ring of Kerry.
- Kenmare is somewhat over 7 miles from this juncture.

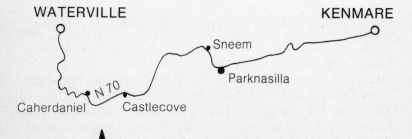

DAY SIX: KENMARE TO KILLARNEY

(20 miles; challenging morning)
We took more pictures on this ride than we can ever remember taking on any previous tour. The ride is only a little over 20 miles, but half of it is up, up, up.

Leave Kenmare north on N71. (sign: Killarney) The incline is slightly uphill for about 1½ miles, then turns more uphill for another 8½ miles. The forested area and heavily rock-strewn fields lead your eye to the stark mountains in the distance. The air is keen and sweet, and was filled with birdsong on the day we rode it. Grass tufts and white stone boulders fill the fields as far as you can see. Continue following N71 all the way to Killarney. We took this route on the Saturday of a holiday weekend in summer, and there was relatively little car traffic. After almost 8 miles the grade turns more steeply uphill; a small lake appears on your right, with more large mountains in the far distance.

After another mile or so, you officially enter Killarney National Park. As you crest the summit, trees begin to appear again, and one of the most spectacular views of the whole tour opens before you. The Ladies View, as it's called, definitely rates a lunch stop. The area got its name from the delighted reaction of Queen Victoria's ladies-in-waiting, who came this way 150 years ago (probably not on bikes, however). There is a fine little café and gift shop here, with a good selection of sandwiches, scones, and such.

It will generally be downhill the rest of the way to Killarney, but it is definitely not scenery to be rushed through. The magnificent vistas change from one perfect tableau to the next so fast that you may think you are watching a slide show of natural beauty. We took a whole roll of pictures on this stretch alone.

A short way down the road you will encounter the ruins of a tower and cross over a bridge above a bubbling stream. Moss covered trees appear on the left as the forest deepens. About 2 miles past the café you'll go into an old rock tunnel and come out just above Lough Leane. The road levels now with some slight ups and downs. Wild pink rhododendrons proliferate as you ride, appearing everywhere on the hills and fields. A bridge over the lake takes you through even taller trees and past a walking trail off to the right. A little over 7 miles down from the summit you'll have the opportunity to visit the Muckross House, one of the area's treasures. Surrounded by gemlike gardens, which you can visit for free, the house itself can be explored for a small fee. It has exhibits of Irish life, various antiquities, plus a friendly tea shop. It is highly renowned and can be quite crowded on the weekends.

Shortly after the Muckross House, you will cross a bridge onto a road with a row of B&Bs as you officially enter **Killarney.**

WHERE TO STAY AND DINE IN KILLARNEY

This is a large town and very busy. Due to the bustle of downtown life, we recommend staying south of town, where it is much quieter.

The Cedar House (tel. [064]32342), operated by Mrs. Carroll, is located near the Gleneagle Hotel and boasts both dinner and high tea. This house is quite luxurious, but is still reasonably priced. (Modest)

The Killarney View House is run by Ms. Mary Guerin (tel. [064]33122); it is a large, riverfront house with fine views. (Modest)

A really good place to eat is Foley's Steak and Seafood Restaurant (tel. [064]31217), with especially good reviews for the fresh fish. (Modest)

A second option, likely to require a reservation, is Linden House (tel. [064]31379), which is a family-run restaurant with a German touch. The food is fresh and substantial. (Modest)

WHAT TO DO IN KILLARNEY

Killarney is a good place to shop, and since it's the end of the tour, you may want to actually buy some of those hand-knit Irish sweaters you've been admiring. Also, you can take a pleasant ride on one of the horse-drawn "jaunting carts" that are parked downtown. If you are heading back to Shannon, you can catch a train here for the short ride back to Limerick.

DAILY SUMMARY

IRELAND TOUR

Day Six: Kenmare to Killarney

(20 miles; challenging morning)

- Leave Kenmare north on N71 (sign: Killarney). The N71 is your road all the way into Killarney.
- The uphill pass is approximately 10 miles, steep for 8½ of that.
- Stay on the main road all the way into Killarney.

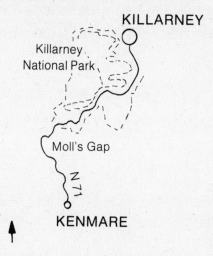

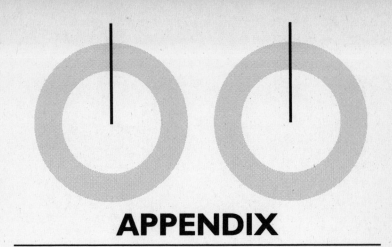

APPENDIX

SELECTED COMPANIES OFFERING BICYCLE TOURS OF GREAT BRITAIN

Backroads Bicycle Touring
1516 5th St.
Berkeley, CA 94710-1740

Travent International
P.O. Box 305
Waterbury Center, VT 05677

Euro-Bike Tours
P.O. Box 40
DeKalb, ILL 60115

Vermont Bicycle Touring
Box 711
Bristol, VT 05443

ⓟ **Plume**

BICYCLE TOURS OF ITALY

by Gay and Kathlyn Hendricks

Savor the rich sights, sounds, and flavors of Italy while enjoying America's fastest growing new sport— bicycle touring. Thousands of adventurous Americans have already traded in the rigors of high-stress, high-cost travel for the fun of biking it to the world's greatest getaways. And now you can do it, too. With this extraordinary guide, you'll learn everything you need to know to put your vacation plans in gear.

There's an epidemic with 27 million victims. And no visible symptoms.

It's an epidemic of people who can't read.

Believe it *or* not, 27 million Americans are functionally illiterate, about one adult in five.

The solution to this problem is you... when you join the fight against illiteracy. So call the Coalition for Literacy at toll-free **1-800-228-8813** and volunteer.

Volunteer Against Illiteracy. The only degree you need is a degree of caring.